LAST OF THE
GLOW WORMS

Last of the Glow Worms

Memoir of a Nuclear Weapons Technician at the End of the Cold War

Jeff Woodward

McFarland & Company, Inc., Publishers
Jefferson, North Carolina

LIBRARY OF CONGRESS CATALOGUING-IN-PUBLICATION DATA

Names: Woodward, Jeff, 1971– author.
Title: Last of the glow worms : memoir of a nuclear weapons technician at the end of the Cold War / Jeff Woodward.
Other titles: Memoir of a nuclear weapons technician at the end of the Cold War
Description: Jefferson, North Carolina : McFarland & Company, Inc., Publishers, 2017 | Includes bibliographical references and index.
Identifiers: LCCN 2017056211 | ISBN 9781476671352 (softcover. : acid free paper) ∞
Subjects: LCSH: Woodward, Jeff, 1971– | Nuclear weapons—United States—History. | Soldiers—United States—Biography. | United States. Army. Ordnance Company, 64th—Biography. | United States. Army—Foreign service—Germany (West)—Anecdotes. | Cold War—Regimental histories—United States. | Nuclear weapons—Maintenance and repair. | Cold War—Personal narratives, American.
Classification: LCC U264 .W68 2017 | DDC 355.0092 [B] —dc23
LC record available at https://lccn.loc.gov/2017056211

BRITISH LIBRARY CATALOGUING DATA ARE AVAILABLE

ISBN (print) 978-1-4766-7135-2
ISBN (ebook) 978-1-4766-3008-3

© 2017 Jeff Woodward. All rights reserved

No part of this book may be reproduced or transmitted in any form or by any means, electronic or mechanical, including photocopying or recording, or by any information storage and retrieval system, without permission in writing from the publisher.

Front cover: Diagram of Pershing II missile (United States Army); background images © 2017 iStock

Manufactured in the United States of America

McFarland & Company, Inc., Publishers
Box 611, Jefferson, North Carolina 28640
www.mcfarlandpub.com

Table of Contents

Preface   1
Introduction   3

1. Getting Out of Dodge   9
2. Learning the Power of the Atom   32
3. Wilkommen in Deutschland   46
4. Working Area One   62
5. Familiar Faces   83
6. Culture Shock   98
7. Nuke Training and Investigations   113
8. Broken Arrow and the NWTI   126
9. Operation *Silent Echo*   141
10. The Final Days of the 64th Ordnance Company   154
11. America or Bust   167

Epilogue   177
References and Further Reading   181
Index   183

Preface

I worked methodically as the Soviet inspector stood to my left, his small, squinted eyes studying me as I removed the neutron generators from the Pershing II missile. This was the first time I had ever met an actual Soviet. The tales we heard of large, burly men ready to destroy capitalism and the American way of life fell short as I gazed upon a medium-built and bushy-eyebrowed stalwart of a beaten empire. I did not gather the courage to speak to him directly (though in retrospect, I can think of hundreds of questions I would have posed to the Soviet). His American counterpart grinned as I looked at him from the corner of my eye. I quickly placed the neutron generators on a tray set aside for the smaller parts being removed from the warhead. The other members of our team were also removing parts from their weapons systems.

Both inspectors seemed to be in a jovial mood, their teams here to watch as the United States upheld its part of the INF (Intermediate-Range Nuclear Forces) Treaty. It was the summer of 1991, and we were in the middle of Operation *Silent Echo*, the Army's designator for the complete disarmament of its nuclear weapons stockpile. This same procedure, removing pieces and bits from warheads that were to be later destroyed in the United States, was happening at every nuclear depot the U.S. Army maintained throughout the world. In Germany, Italy, Turkey, South Korea, Greece and the mainland United States, the other soldiers classified in our MOS (military occupational specialty 55G, nuclear weapons specialists), or, as we were so affectionately called among the artillery units, "glow worms," were doing the same thing.

During the twilight of the Cold War, the United States maintained an estimated 10,000 nuclear capable missiles and artillery shells, while the Soviet Union's arsenal was estimated at 11,000. The arms race, and the concept of "self-assured mutual destruction," a term coined by scientist John von Neumann during the 1950s, kept the leaders of the United States and the Soviet Union from pushing the dreaded red button. When the 1980s came to a close, and with the dissolution of the Soviet Union and the Warsaw Pact, the threat of this so-called mutual destruction diminished significantly. For those of us growing up during the Cold War, the threat was real and always a subconscious worry. The era of Glasnost and Perestroika changed the world, and the threat shifted from the superpower arms race, to smaller, rogue nations trying to acquire the technology to develop the same weapons of mass destruction.

This is an account of just one of these nuclear weapons soldiers, these glow worms, who played a pivotal role at the end of the Cold War but are among the least known of America's atomic soldiers.

Introduction

Americans love war stories. They love to read about the men and women in the military who are extraordinary, the soldiers who defy the term "regular" and go above and beyond the call of duty.

Sergeant Alvin York, who during World War I single-handedly killed 28 German soldiers and captured 132 others, captured the hearts of Americans during the 1920s. General George Patton, whose personality and grit made him a legend during the Second World War, is still a popular figure to study. The war stories of infantrymen, Marines, LAARPs and Special Forces soldiers who dripped blood, sweat and tears during the Vietnam conflict are numerous and are sought after by military enthusiasts.

Americans also love war heroes. They immerse themselves in their stories and imagine themselves in the heat of battle, bullets whizzing by overhead, as the hero low crawls around the still-warm bodies of his fallen comrades, outnumbered and almost out of ammunition, but defying the odds and placing the explosives at the enemy ammo dump to complete the mission.

These are the stories we love. The tales of a soldier up against seemingly impossible odds and emerging victorious. But not all military stories pertain to war. Some are of the men and women working behind the scenes, performing a duty just as important as the brave soul on the front line.

This is the true story of my journey from high school student to experienced nuke tech, all before the age of 21.

I never deployed to a combat zone; I never shot at an enemy or had a grenade thrown at me. I never drove a tank or fired a Stinger Missile; I never had to stop the bleeding of a wounded comrade or call in an airstrike on an enemy target.

Introduction

The mission performed by nuclear weapons technicians during the Cold War are nonetheless just as important. There are no books written about them, no movies made, and no medals handed out. They were behind the scenes, performing maintenance on the Army's tactical nuclear warhead arsenal around the world, from the Korean Peninsula to Europe. Men and women, some still teenagers, were given top-secret clearances to perform their duties as MOS 55Gs. This duty was performed until 1992, with the final destruction of all U.S. Army tactical nuclear warheads.

During the 1980s, no one foresaw the impending collapse of the Soviet Union and the Warsaw Pact, and our movie heroes reflected it. Cartoonish characters were introduced to us through the likes of Sylvester Stallone, Chuck Norris and Arnold Schwarzenegger, who were all more than willing to take out Russians with an M60 machine gun that never ran out of bullets.

Red Dawn came out in 1984, and viewers were introduced to an alternative history. What if the Soviet Union invaded the United States? The premise was older than the year 1984, but this was the first time that moviegoers witnessed a well-cast movie that brought the premise to life.

The movie that changed the face of the Cold War aired on November 20, 1983. *The Day After* focuses on life in a small Kansas town after a full-scale nuclear exchange between the United States and the Soviet Union. Nuclear fallout, radiation sickness and societal collapse are all imagined in the movie. One hundred million Americans watched it when it aired, making it the highest rated TV movie in history. *The Day After* even had an effect on policymakers, and the INF Treaty was signed by President Ronald Reagan just four years later.

The mood of film and music throughout the Western world revolved around the possibility of nuclear war, with songs such as Nena's "99 Luftballons" topping the charts in the West. It was a real-life threat that most people pushed to the back of their minds as they tried to live their everyday lives.

The use of bomb shelters and bunkers, which were popular during the 1950s, fell out of style by the 1980s. In the late 1970s until the mid–1980s, we had drills in school pertaining to a nuclear detonation. They usually happened on Tuesday mornings, and we had to scramble to get underneath our wooden desks at the sound of the air siren and cover our heads. School "scare" films, the old black and white movies from

Introduction

the 1950s, were shown, such as *Duck and Cover*. It seemed so normal at the time.

Most libraries and county buildings had the unmistakable black and yellow placards adhered to the outside facades of their buildings indicating a fallout shelter that could be used by the public in the event of a nuclear detonation. New York City had fallout shelters in the concrete pylons of bridges, stocked with non-perishable food, toiletries, and potable water. That is how real the threat felt to Americans.

In 1983, NATO held the training exercise called Able Archer 83. The purpose of the exercise was to simulate East-West tensions that culminate in a nuclear exchange between the Soviet Union and the United States. What made the 1983 exercise different from previous exercises was the participation of heads of state. The Soviets were alarmed, believing the exercise was a ruse, and NATO was planning a nuclear first strike. The Soviets put aircraft in East Germany and Poland on alert to counter the perceived attack. Their fears were alleviated when the exercise ended ten days later.

Nineteen eighty-three was a year of great tension between the two superpowers. The Soviet Union mistakenly shot down Korean Airlines flight 007, killing American Congressman Larry McDonald. Pershing II nuclear ballistic missiles were deployed throughout Europe to counter the Soviet deployment of SS-20 Saber nuclear missiles in the Ukrainian Soviet Socialist Republic, which were capable of striking Brussels. But the one event that brought the adversaries to the brink of real nuclear war occurred on September 26, 1983. The Soviet nuclear early warning system reported multiple launches of USAF Minuteman nuclear ICBMs, and the quick thinking of Lieutenant Colonel Stanislav Petrov, who correctly identified that the alarm was a fault in a new satellite system installed by the Soviet military. Petrov's failure to report the incident to the Soviet High Command assuredly saved the two nations from nuclear destruction.

The U.S. Army focused on the strategy of tactical nuclear weapons when it came to the defense of Europe. The M422, which was an eight-inch nuclear projectile produced in the 1950s and still part of the nuclear arsenal until 1992, was one of the first artillery fired nuclear weapons ever developed. Along with the M454 nuclear projectile, these two systems were well known to 55Gs from the 1960s until the phasing out of the MOS.

Earlier systems that were familiar to Army nuke techs included the M31 Honest John and the MGM-29 Sergeant.

The Honest John was the first nuclear capable surface-to-surface missile in the U.S. Army's arsenal. The missile had a range of 15 miles carrying a 20-kiloton warhead. It was also able to carry clusters of Sarin nerve gas canisters as a payload. The system was replaced by the MGM-52 Lance missile system, and the last Honest John missiles were removed from Europe in 1985.

The MGM-29 Sergeant was a nuclear surface-to-surface missile deployed by the U.S. Army in South Korea and Europe in 1963. The missile had a range between 25 and 84 miles and was outfitted to carry a 200-kiloton nuclear warhead. Like the Honest John, the Sergeant was replaced by the Lance missile system and removed from service in the late 1970s.

One of the more controversial nuclear weapons systems developed by the U.S. Army was the SADM (Special Atomic Demolition Munition). The SADM was developed in the 1960s as a man-portable nuclear device that could be deployed behind Soviet lines in the event of an invasion of Western Europe. It had a nuclear yield of .02 to one kiloton. A team would parachute behind enemy lines and deploy the SADM to destroy power plants and bridges and to disrupt enemy communications. In *Code Name: Copperhead*, written by Sergeant Major Joe Garner, a retired Special Forces soldier, Garner describes his jump with a SADM in a training exercise at Fort Bragg, the first of its kind. A second parachutist would jump with the first to provide support. The U.S. Army created an MOS, 12E, SADM Specialist, who was also trained to deploy the weapon. The 12E would be supported by a 55G nuclear weapons specialist. The MOS 12E was eliminated from the Army in 1986.

During my time at the 64th Ordnance Company, we were custodians of four weapons systems, two artillery-fired and two missile systems. We knew the systems were dispersed at various depots in Germany, Italy, Greece and Turkey. Before the advent of the Internet, we had little to no contact with the other depots in Germany, let alone those in southern Europe, Turkey or Korea.

After the fall of the Berlin Wall in 1989 and the collapse of the Soviet Union the following year, the threat of nuclear war waned. The United States and Russia still upheld the INF Treaty after 1991, and as

Introduction

Russia struggled with economic reforms, the United States focused on Iraq and the rising tide of Islamic extremism throughout the Middle East. The times had changed, and the old guard made way for a new American strategy, less focused on nuclear deterrence and more concentrated on non-national conflicts and urban warfare.

The photographs of Area One, the nuclear storage site, were taken in the years *after* the depot had deactivated. Cameras were not allowed past the entrance gate to Area Two, and we were searched daily before entrance to Area One. The photographs of Area One in this book were taken by a group of Germans shortly after the closing of the depot. They have an interest in keeping the legacy of nuclear armament in Germany alive, in the form of photographic documentation and land protection, allowing them to turn the former depot into a Cold War memorial.

1
Getting Out of Dodge

I always knew I was going to join the military. It was my calling. It was a part of who I was. I made this revelation one summer day in 1986, as the Vietnam Moving Wall Memorial was passing through Chicago. I went with my father, who served with the 9th Infantry Division in Dong Tam in 1967–1968. He never spoke of the war, but he had frequent nightmares (when he wasn't passed out drunk), and little green dots caused by shrapnel from a mortar shell fired by the Viet Cong peppered his chest. This is what he brought back from Vietnam: an alcohol problem and green-colored scars caused by an enemy he could not see.

I was very proud to stand next to him, as he met and spoke with other Vietnam veterans, especially those that wore the 9th Infantry Division patch. I had never heard him speak so openly about his experiences in the war, and it could only be done with those who understood what he experienced and how he felt as a veteran who was cast aside after his arrival to the mainland after his deployment. I watched him stand there, tears in his eyes as he walked up and down the length of the Wall. I wanted that feeling too. The sense of patriotism. The sense of duty to country. I wanted those feelings, and my mind was set on how to get them. I was 14 years old and knew where I was going to start life after high school. It was the Army.

I attended a Catholic school in Brookfield, Illinois, from the first through the eighth grades, but since money was tight in our household, I had to attend a public high school. This meant leaving the relative security of a private school with a total eighth grade class of 18, to a freshman class that had more than 900 students. I was in culture shock, and in the fall of 1985, I learned quickly what a jock, skid, preppy and goth were. I also learned what a dork was, and I fell into this category almost immediately. This meant that I also had a target on my back. I tried to keep to myself and ignore the taunts from bigger students. The bullying went on consistently my freshman year, but when I entered my sophomore year it seemed the jocks either ran out of steam or developed other hobbies, such as chasing girls. I didn't question the change and focused on more important matters, like getting a driver's license and a job. In between, I read a lot, mostly fantasy and science fiction books. The books were my escape, and I always enjoyed stories with a strong hero, a quest, or a mission to accomplish against almost insurmountable odds. This was the way I wanted to see myself, not as the kid who would get gum thrown at him in the hallway.

My junior year began with me finally being able to see the Army recruiter. I drove to his office after school one day in October 1987, a few days after my 16th birthday. The office was located in a small, plain brick-faced strip mall in Countryside, Illinois. I entered the office and took a seat in the waiting room. There were pamphlets strewn about across the end tables, Combat Arms, the Montgomery G.I. Bill, Skills for the Future: the United States Army. I skimmed through the Combat Arms pamphlet, which briefly summarized the various combat-based MOSs (military occupational specialty): infantry, artillery, air cavalry. The photos depicted men in camouflage, with their faces painted in green and black, holding various weapons. I focused on their faces, trying to determine if they actually enjoy being infantrymen or were posing strictly for the camera.

"May I help you, son?"

I dropped the pamphlet and looked at the man standing in front of me. He was wearing his Class A dress uniform. The ribbons on his chest were brightly colored and lined up in three horizontal rows. He had an expert infantry badge just above his ribbons, and the recognizable light-blue rope that circled from his shoulder around his underarm was unmistakably infantry. His hair was neatly parted to the left, and a small, pencil-thin mustache hovered just above his upper lip. He seemed to be in his mid–30s and he had the look of an experienced Army veteran.

"I am interested in joining the Army, sir," I responded. I stood and he held out his hand. I took it and thought his hand was rather soft for a soldier. "I was hoping you can give some information about what the army has to offer."

1. Getting Out of Dodge

"My name is Sergeant Averson. The reference 'Sir' is reserved for officers. Do you know the difference?"

I squinted. "No, not really."

"Well, come into my office, and I'll explain the difference." I followed the sergeant into his office and sat down in a comfortable leather chair. He sat down directly opposite of me and began his pitch. I could tell instantly that the speech was well-rehearsed and had probably been made hundreds of times to other young men and women who were interested in signing up. True to his word, he began by explaining the difference between enlisted men and officers, who would be called "Sir" or "Ma'am," and how to address NCOs (non-commissioned officers). He covered the basics of the rank structure, life in the Army, and the benefits of enlisting. I only nodded my head as he continued, absorbing everything he said with enthusiasm. Sergeant Averson was very good at what he did, and at the end of our first meeting, I agreed to take the ASVAB (Armed Services Vocational Aptitude Battery), the test given to all new recruits for any of the military branches. The next test was being held the following Saturday at the MEPS (Military Entrance Processing Station) in Des Plaines, Illinois, at 8 a.m. Sergeant Averson informed me that he would be driving me there, as there were two other interested students who would also be taking the test. I rose from my seat and shook Averson's hand, grabbed a couple of pamphlets from the table and drove home.

My parents were rather ambivalent about me considering the Army as a choice after high school. I thought my father would have been more receptive given his military experience, but he seemed rather subdued about the concept. My mother was always busy with work and taking care of my three younger brothers, and I believed it would have been more of a relief for her if I left. They did not have the money to send me to college, and a family of four boys drained funds, though I did not realize it at the time. I told them I was taking the ASVAB the next Saturday morning, and they both just nodded and got back to what they were doing. At that moment I realized I had to do well on the test. It was either that or end up working a minimum wage job somewhere in the city. All of what Sergeant Averson said to me about the benefits of being in the military rushed back to me and my mood lightened.

I was going to make it.

Last of the Glow Worms

True to his word, Sergeant Averson picked me up on Saturday morning at 6:30. I sat in the back seat, as there were two other prospective recruits in the car. I nodded hello at them, and we drove off. Des Plaines was about 45 minutes from my house, so we began talking about what MOSs we were interested in.

"Infantry," said Prospective Recruit Number One. He was sitting in passenger seat of the car. He looked to be 19 and rather husky. Spittle flew from his mouth as he spoke. "I wanna be on the frontlines, running and shooting." He said this very matter-of-factly, which caused me to smirk. He went on about wanting to shoot machine guns, fire rocket launchers, toss hand grenades, and about becoming the new Rambo, you know, so he could kill Russians and get all the women he wanted. When he stopped, I just sat there speechless.

After a few moments of silence, Prospective Recruit Number 2, who was sitting next to me in the back seat, began to speak.

"I want to be a tank driver. That's it. I want to drive tanks." I waited for more, but nothing else came out of him. He turned his head and looked out of the car window. I didn't press him or ask any questions. That was it. The boy just wanted to drive tanks.

"And you, Woodward?" asked Sergeant Averson. "What MOS are you interested in?"

I realized then I had no answer. Sure, I would love to drive tanks. And I sure as hell want to shoot machine guns, or fire rocket launchers, just like every other 16-year-old boy in America would want to do, but it seemed to me that there was much more to the Army than just shooting guns.

"I don't know yet, sergeant; I just want to take the test first." The other boys in the car laughed, but I saw Sergeant Averson crack a small grin in the rearview mirror.

I later realized this was a grin of approval, not of mirth.

The test began at 8 sharp. We were told that each section would be timed and would be covering areas such as math, electronics, vocabulary, etc. The room was packed with about 40 prospective recruits and was very diversified. The men in uniform who were administering the test asked for quiet and told us to begin section one of the test. The room quieted down, and we began. The room was completely silent except for the scratching of pencils as they filled in the little circles of the scan cards. We had one short break about halfway through the test

1. Getting Out of Dodge

and finished three hours later. We handed in our last scan card, the testers thanked us for coming, and we shuffled out of the room.

Sergeant Averson was waiting for me in the hallway. Prospective Recruits One and Two were already with him. The sergeant took us for lunch after the test, then drove us home. He spoke most of the way home, mostly about life in the Army. I was the first to be dropped off. He said that the test scores should be ready in a few days, and he would contact me as soon as he had them.

It was the longest two days of my life.

I received the call from Sergeant Averson the following Tuesday morning. He asked me to come into his office after school to go over the test results. I was on the work program at school, which meant I got out of school at 2 p.m. and started at my job at 4. Elated, I told him I would be there at 2:15.

When I entered Sergeant Averson's office, I was surprised to see another soldier sitting there. He was dressed in his Class As and wore captain bars on his lapel. I learned from Sergeant Averson to address officers as "Sir," which I did when I entered the room.

"Hello, Jeff, please sit down," Sergeant Averson greeted me warmly. Pointing to the captain he said, "This is Captain Banks. He will be sitting in on this meeting." I glanced warily at the captain. I had never met an officer before and was a little apprehensive. The sergeant noticed my discomfort.

"It's okay, Jeff. The captain is only here to observe my performance." The sergeant cast a quick wink at me. "I'm up for promotion, so make me look good." I let out a brief laugh, then quickly composed myself. I had an odd feeling that the recruiter was not telling me the full truth. Sergeant Averson began.

"We got your testing results back. How would you like to be a cook?" I looked at the sergeant in confusion.

"Um, a cook?" I was at a loss for words. What would my father think?

The sergeant looked at me, then looked down at his paper, then looked back at me again, smiling. "You tested well in the culinary arts, so I thought I would throw that out there." His smile widened. "But you also tested well in general science and engineering. In fact, extremely well. This leaves the choice of enlisted MOSs wide open." He pushed away the test results and looked at a paper that was lying underneath.

"There is an opening in an MOS that doesn't come along very

often. The MOS is 55G, or Nuclear Weapons Technician. The function of a 55G is the maintenance and handling of nuclear warheads and nuclear capable artillery shells." He stopped reading to look up at my face. I must have had a smile from ear to ear, because he smiled back at me, put his head down, and continued reading. "This MOS will require a top-secret security clearance, which means that background checks and interviews with references by the Department of Defense. Pending the outcome of the background checks and interviews, you will be enlisted in the U.S. Army as a 55G." The sergeant paused to let me soak everything in. My head was spinning with excitement. He continued.

"This MOS also offers a bonus of station of choice. 55Gs are stationed in the continental United States, various countries in Europe, and South Korea. In addition, you will be eligible for the Montgomery G.I. Bill for college assistance, after completing a mandatory time of service. The minimum enlistment term for MOS 55G is three years."

Sergeant Averson stopped speaking and looked at me. I knew he was finished and waiting for an answer. The captain sat silently; he hadn't said a word during the exchange. I could hardly contain my excitement, and the sergeant probably knew it.

Without hesitation, I responded. "Sign me up."

The following weekend, Sergeant Averson came to my house with the paperwork. My mother and father sat in the living with us, and we all huddled around a small coffee table in front of the couch. Since I was still 16 years old, I could not legally enlist in the military without parental consent. I would sign my name on page after page, and my father would sign his right below mine. They were all legal formalities that every new recruit had to sign, with the exception of the background check that needed to be performed for the security clearance. I had to write down five references that would be contacted and sign my initials after each of their names. I wrote down names of the older guys I worked with at an engine shop a few blocks away. I didn't want to trust the interviews to my friends or acquaintances.

The last page that needed to be signed was the station of choice. I had to pick three stations, starting with the station I wanted the most. I picked Germany as my first station, Greece as my second, and South Korea as my third. After signing my name a final time, Sergeant Averson stacked the papers neatly and put them in his briefcase. The following

1. Getting Out of Dodge

Saturday I would have to go back to the MEPS station for an initial physical. If the physical and background check had no problems, then I would be cleared to leave. My entry date would be July 26, 1989.

The FBI came to my house the following week after I passed my entrance physical. They were dressed in stereotypical black suits, but I did not see any sunglasses. I would have chuckled to myself about this observation, but I was too nervous to think about anything except what they were going to ask. They sat on the couch, my mother sat in the reclining chair, and I sat on the floor. She offered them coffee, and they refused. They would only take a few minutes of our time. I wished my father was present, but he was at work. One of the agents pulled some paperwork out of his briefcase, and began. They explained my rights first, and if anything was found to be fabricated or untrue, I would not be granted a security clearance.

"Do you understand your rights, Jeff?"

"Yes, sir, I do."

"Then let's begin."

Are you a gang member? Are you a homosexual? Do you support the communist party? Are you party to any lawsuit involving the United States government? Have you ever done drugs, including marijuana? Are you willing to hold sensitive information, including confidential, secret and top-secret without exposing it to unqualified individuals? The questions kept coming, and I began to relax. Most of the questions had nothing to do with a 16-year-old boy, they were geared more for a 25-year-old college student.

The interview came to an end sooner than I had expected. After the barrage of questions, I was mentally drained. The agents packed up their paperwork, shook my hand, and left. I was elated the interview went well, and afterward went to my room to soak it all in.

One step closer.

I was at work a couple of days later, when the men I wrote in as references were called to the boss's office. One by one, they were pulled into another, smaller office by the same FBI agents to ask questions about me. I was scared and started second-guessing my choices of references. What if one of them decided to railroad me, and not by accident? Or maybe by accident? What if they answered a question wrong, or lied to the agents? My mind was flipping, and I could barely concentrate on my work.

Forty-five minutes later, the last of the three co-workers came back to work. The FBI agents did not speak with me, and after they left I drilled my co-workers on what was asked and was what said.

Is Jeff a gang member? Is he homosexual? Has he ever spoken badly about the United States government? How does he perform at work? Does have any questionable friends or acquaintances? Is he a communist? I almost doubled over in laughter.

They were the exact same questions I had been asked.

I got teased a lot for signing up for the military. Mostly from friends who were going to hang around the neighborhood and try to find union jobs. I believed that I was made for something more than driving a forklift on a dock for a trucking company or driving scrapers and bulldozers for Local 150. It was just something I felt inside of me.

At work I was treated differently. The older men began to treat me like an adult, and some of the guys who were in the military in their younger years began to congratulate me on enlisting. The owner even gave me a raise to $4.00 an hour. Working 20 hours a week during the school year and bringing home $50 per week had me feeling like a junior Rockefeller.

To celebrate my enlistment, I took my youngest brother and his friends to an Italian restaurant in Brookfield named Enzos. There, I let them pick out anything on the menu, which ended up being a large pizza and a pitcher of Coke for all of them. I paid for the entire meal and felt good about spending some quality time with my youngest brother, who was having a hard time dealing with my leaving.

The anticipation of leaving was so great, graduation seemed to take longer to arrive than it actually did. After going to the prom and spending the weekend in South Haven, Michigan, and the pomp and circumstance of graduation, school for me was officially over.

I spent my weekends after graduation with Sergeant Averson and a few other kids from school who signed up for the Army. He would drive us to Fort Sheridan, in Highland Park, Illinois, and we would watch the soldiers' PT (physical training) on the parade grounds. We would also train in basic drill, like marching, then go over the code of conduct and general orders. Sergeant Averson told us we would be learning all of this in detail at basic training, but he didn't want us to walk in blindly. He would also take us into the PX (post exchange) to look around. The PX on Fort Sheridan looked like any other grocery

1. Getting Out of Dodge

store. I was expecting to find the shelves stocked with ammunition, rifles and MREs. When I saw loaves of bread, canned goods and televisions, I realized the soldiers stationed here were taken care of and had a life outside of soldiering.

July 26 came quickly, and on the morning of my departure to the MEPS station, I checked and rechecked my small gym bag to make sure I had everything that I needed: toothbrush, deodorant, two pairs of underwear, two white undershirts, one pair of jeans and two pairs of socks. I did not shave yet, so I did not pack a razor and shaving cream, also on the list of items to bring.

Sergeant Averson would be taking me to the MEPS station, and I paced nervously in the living room while I waited. My three brothers and mother were there; my father was at work. The night before, he hugged me and said to be careful and to follow directions. He also gave the sage advice that was given to him when he was enlisted: "Don't volunteer for anything." I did not understand what he meant until much later in my military career.

When the sergeant arrived, he honked the horn for me to come out. I hugged my mother; she had tears in her eyes and told me to be careful. I gave my brothers hugs also and noticed the youngest of them was crying. Seeing him there, nine years old, hair disheveled and not a care in the world, also brought me to tears. I hugged him tightly and told him I would call him as soon as I had a chance. The goodbyes still hanging in the living room air, I grabbed my bag and jumped into Sergeant Averson's car.

"Ready?" he asked.

"Ready," I answered without hesitation.

The next day, I would be at Fort Dix, New Jersey.

I had only flown once before, and that was to Washington, D.C., as an eighth grade graduation present from my grandmother. I had feared it and the flight to New Jersey was no different. I kept imagining the plane losing its power and going into a freefall at 32,000 feet. Acrophobia stayed with me throughout my life, so much so that my legs would become paralyzed with fear just going up an escalator. Like the first time I flew, my fear was unwarranted. We landed safely at Newark in the early evening and were herded to the pick-up area outside of the terminal. There were hundreds of recruits scurrying around, trying to find the correct buses. I stuck with the group that flew from Chicago and followed it, since a few of those recruits seemed to be older than me and I felt inclined to latch on to them. The soldiers standing outside of the buses began to shout commands.

Women in the first two buses, men in the last four buses! Line up! Move, move, move!

I followed the rest and got in line. In orderly fashion we entered the buses. I was near the end of the line, and when I stepped on the bus, most of the seats were taken. I ended up sitting directly behind the bus driver, who kept a smile on his face, but otherwise remained silent during the trip. The other recruits were talking amongst themselves, some louder than others. I came to a quick realization that the loud guys were the ones who believed themselves to be in charge. They were the ones talking loudly so that everyone could hear them and would be the ones who kissed ass to get promoted. I took this all in and kept quiet the short ride to Fort Dix.

Fort Dix was a staging ground for World War I soldiers assigned to the 78th, 87th and 34th Divisions. After the war, it served as a demobilization center. When World War II began, Fort Dix once again assumed its role as a staging and training ground for soldiers heading to the European Theater. After the war, Fort Dix became a basic training facility for new recruits and home to the 9th Infantry Division. The 9th moved out in 1954, and Fort Dix became home to the 69th Infantry Division. After the 69th was deactivated in 1956, the fort focused on its basic training program.

We arrived at the reception center just after 11 p.m. At the entrance of the building was a red painted container with the words "Amnesty Box."

A specialist stood in front of the building and said in a loud voice, "If you have any contraband, put it in the box now. This includes weapons, drugs, cigarettes, and lighters. Anything found in your possession after this point will be considered an offense." Some recruits went to the box and dropped items into it. I waited until their turn was up and walked there myself to put a lighter into the opening.

We were then hustled to our rooms, which were small, two-man abodes that contained a bunk bed. My roommate for the evening was another young man like myself whose name was Jim. Jim was a 55B (ammunition handler). He also liked to talk. He went on about Sioux City, Iowa, his hometown, how many brothers and sisters he had, why

1. Getting Out of Dodge

he joined the military, his GPA in high school, and his religion. When he finally tired of speaking, it was well past midnight, and I felt I knew more about Jim than the Army did.

Morning came fast, and I was still groggy when we were called out of our rooms. We were told we had five minutes to brush our teeth, shave, and get into formation for chow. I ran to the latrine, which had eight mirrors and sinks, and a row of stalls. I brushed my teeth, together with fifteen other recruits, ran back to the room and grabbed my bag. I then rushed to the front of the building, where a formation had been started. This was when I learned to *never* be last to a formation. We waited as our names were called, and the sergeant in charge of the formation realized a few recruits were missing. He began to yell about being prompt and selected two volunteers to run back into the building to find the stragglers. Just as soon as they entered, they returned with the four missing recruits. The sergeant began to scream at them and then ordered them into a front leaning rest position. I had no idea what he meant, and I am sure the stragglers had no idea either.

Get in the front leaning rest position, privates! Do y'all know what a push up is? Get down!

The privates dropped to the ground, and the sergeant began to count as they pushed their bodies up and down.

One, two, three, ONE!

One, two, three, TWO!

The privates had to say the numbers loud on the last count as they did their push-ups. I found out that very first day that two push-ups in the civilian world actually add up to one push-up in the Army. After they reached ten, they were told to get back in formation. I fought the urge to look at them and kept my head forward.

Pick up your bags!

We picked them up.

Right face, huh!

We turned to the right. Sergeant Averson's pre-basic training saved me, and I noticed that most of the other recruits also had some sort of pre-training. Those that didn't were in a hard spot, and the front leaning rest position taught them soon enough.

Forward, huh!

We started to march, though I had no idea where we were going. We kept in rhythm with the sergeant's methodical voice.

Your left, your left, your left, right!

He kept at it, and we began to sing cadences as we marched. I noticed this helped keep my mind from focusing on marching. We cadenced about everything from mamas to the Vietnam war. The march lasted for 25 minutes, until we stood in formation in front of the mess hall. We got into a single file line and began the slow process of entering the building. As we entered, we had to shout out our last name and last four digits of our social security number to the old man sitting at a desk to the right of the entrance.

The mess hall looked like a school cafeteria, only with more confusion. It was loud, with the clinking of glasses and plates from hundreds of soldiers. I took my place in line and jostled forward with the rest. I took a tray, and we were told to put two empty glasses on it, along with a fork, knife and spoon. We shuffled in line to where the food was being given out, cafeteria style. The first woman behind the counter gave me two pancakes. I shuffled to my left, and the second woman gave me some hash browns and scrambled eggs. I again shuffled, and at the end of the line, there was a machine that dispensed milk, orange juice, Kool-Aid or water. I filled the two glasses with orange juice and looked for a place to sit. I then heard the sergeant yell.

Five minutes! Y'all have five minutes, and clear those plates!

I was always a relatively fast eater, but I never had to shovel in food as fast as I had to that morning. I ate the pancakes dry with no butter or syrup and washed then down with one of the glasses of orange juice. The hash browns and eggs were lukewarm, which made them much harder to get down. I pushed myself to eat them, and the second glass of orange juice quickly followed. I leaped out of my chair just in time for the sergeant to scream again.

Let's go, let's go, let's go! Trays away! Formation outside!

I set my tray with the other dirty dishes and ran outside. We waited quietly for a few minutes in formation, then some stragglers came out. The sergeant dropped them. After push-ups, we began to march again. We marched passed barracks and a PX, and we saw several box trucks with very tiny windows pass us by. These were the infamous "cattle cars" used to transport recruits from one area of the base to another. After a mile of marching, we stopped in front of one of the barracks. In front of the formation stood three soldiers. Two of them were older men wearing the well-recognized round-brimmed hat of a drill sergeant. The other

1. Getting Out of Dodge

was a woman wearing an Australian-looking hat with the left side of the brim folded upward. One of the drill sergeants began to address us.

"Gentlemen! Welcome to Fort Dix. I am Staff Sergeant Benson. This is Staff Sergeant Skraggs, and that nice woman to my left is Staff Sergeant Rendels. You all are now part of Company B, First Battalion, 26th Infantry Regiment. We will be your trainers for the next eight weeks. Not all of you will make it through. Some of you will quit. That is why we are here. To help those who do not want to be here quit. You have ten minutes to get to your bunks and drop your civilian bags and be back in formation! Move, move, move!"

All 221 recruits ran into the barracks. We were called by last names and sent to our rooms. I ended up in a small, two-man room with a bunk bed and a window overlooking the courtyard behind the building. I heard a voice behind me and realized my new roommate had walked in. To my surprise, it was Jim from the reception station.

We marched in formation to the reception center, where we lined up by platoon. We were first sent to the barber for our buzzcuts. The reason the military shaves the heads of new recruits is to prevent the spread of lice, if one happens to be infested. From the barber, we headed to the supply building for our uniforms. We were issued three complete sets of BDUs (battle dress uniforms), which were camouflage green, head cover, five sets of thick, olive-drab socks, five pairs of underwear, five brown tee shirts, a belt and a pair of black combat boots. These we conveniently stored in our Army-issue duffle bag, which we then carried to the infirmary. There, we lined up for immunizations and had a quick physical. The recruits that wore or needed glasses were sent to receive their wide-rimmed specs.

We spent the rest of the day getting our gear, which included our Kevlar helmet, poncho, shelter half, gas mask, mess kit, LBV (load bearing vest), rucksack and NBC (nuclear, biological, chemical) gear. After our gear was issued, it was time to march to the mess hall for dinner. Once again it was a madhouse, yelling out last names and social security numbers, grabbing a tray, and rushing to eat. After chow, we once again marched to the barracks. We loaded our gear into our wall lockers and prepared of lights out. My roommate Jim rambled on about nothing in particular from the bottom bunk, but my mind was elsewhere.

I was 17 years old, fresh out of high school, and I had survived my first day of boot camp.

I soon discovered that 99 percent of all the recruits in my company were non-combat arms type MOSs. There were a lot of ammunition handlers, truck drivers, mechanics and TOW missile repairmen in addition to two other nuclear weapon technicians like myself. I say 99 percent, because one recruit in the whole company was a combat arms MOS. He turned out to be an 11C or combat mortarman. When the drill sergeants learned this, they seemed elated. One of their own was at Fort Dix for basic training, instead of Fort Benning or Fort Knox, which were geared more toward the infantry types. They harped on him at first, yelling about how easy he had it compared to his other infantry brothers, but I noticed from there on out they kept a close eye on him, giving him the extra attention to help him through.

Basic training at Fort Dix was divided into three phases: Red, White and Blue. We just entered Red Phase, and our company was ready. The first week of Red Phase consisted almost entirely of marching drills and Army etiquette. Each morning began with PT, in which we did calisthenics in the company grounds, which was followed by a three-mile run. Breakfast always came after PT, then after a short clean up, it was back to formation in front of the barracks. We marched back and forth around the company area, practicing to stay in step, all the while the drill sergeants were screaming at those who had no rhythm and dropping those who failed to listen. I learned quickly to pay attention and not ask questions. I also learned that punishment was communal; when one recruit screwed up, we all had to pay the price, usually with the front leaning rest position until muscle failure.

Red Phase also consisted of learning basic first aid techniques, commo (communications over radio), and BRM (basic rifle marksmanship). I was definitely waiting to fire the M16. We were issued our rifles, but Red Phase consisted only of disassembling and reassembling them. I learned the M16 inside and out and loved the feel of it in my hands. It was lightweight and balanced, and it rested easily on the shoulder when marching. It made me feel like a man.

The M16 is an iconic weapon, representative of an American soldier. It had been in use since the Vietnam conflict, and despite early functional problems, the weapon had become a reliable rifle after revisions were made.

Weighing just nine pounds fully loaded, the M16 is a versatile battlefield rifle, designed for battles in the 300–400 meter range, with a

1. Getting Out of Dodge

maximum effective range of 550 meters. The rifle has a selector switch, allowing the soldier the select between "safe," "semi-automatic" and "full auto" mode. With the adoption of the M16A2 by the U.S. Army in the late 1980s, the select fire mode was changed to "safe," "semi auto" and "burst," which when selected causes the rifle to fire a three-round burst. In basic training, the M16A1 is still used.

During these first two weeks, we had four recruits drop out. I also watched as some went on profile (medical restrictions) for various reasons (stomach problems, headaches, blisters on their feet, etc.). I also had blisters on my feet from marching in new boots, but I sucked it up. I had nowhere else to go.

One of the recruits who dropped out told me that he had made a mistake by joining the military. He was 18 years old and wanted to get away from the poverty of his neighborhood in Detroit. He knew if he stayed there he would end up either in a gang and dead or working at a minimum wage job but alive. He confided in me that he missed his family, specifically his mother, and he wanted to go home.

I watched day after day as he fell out of formations and vomited on the hot concrete. The drill sergeants would yell at him and circle his shaking frame, until finally relenting and sending him to sick call. When he would get back to the barracks, he would stay in his bunk and not come out of his room. At this point, I could not tell if he was playing the part of a legitimately sick soldier or if he had subconsciously convinced himself that he really was ill. Night after night of keeping to himself he finally convinced the Army that he was not fit to be a soldier. I watched him the day he left, carrying a duffel bag full of his belongings to a waiting car, when he turned with a smile and waved to the barracks, and at no one in particular, before he drove off and returned to civilian life.

White Phase began in the third week. We were now allowed to go to the range and live fire our M16s. The morning we were loaded into the cattle cars to go to the range, I could barely contain my excitement. It must have been 105 degrees in the back of the truck, everyone packed together carrying all their gear, but I didn't care. I was about to fire a rifle for the first time. We arrived late morning and were herded from the trucks.

We formed up and were marched by platoon to our respective spots on the range. There we would fire at targets between 25 and 75 meters away. The targets were controlled and would pop up at varying distances. With excitement I took the prone position in my lane and attached the brass deflector to the ejection port of the rifle, since I shot left-handed. We waited for the rangemaster to call out, "Take one 20 round magazine and put it in the rifle!" I took the magazine from my ammo pouch on my LBV, slapped it on my helmet, then inserted it into the rifle.

"Platoon, lock and load!" I pulled the charging handle back, which chambered a round.

"Set your rifles from safe to semi-automatic!" I switched the selector, which was probably one of the most beautiful sounds I had ever heard.

"Platoon, prepare to fire!" I waited until I saw a target pop up 75 meters out. I took aim and fired, completely focused on knocking down the target. One by one, the targets popped up at 25, 50 or 75 meters. The "popping" of the rounds being fired is unnerving at first, and after three rounds of targets, I became more in tune with the firing going on around me. As our platoon fired, another platoon would keep track of the hits. My first time out, I scored a 32 out of 40, which qualified me for the sharpshooter badge.

In addition to live firing, White Phase also sent us out on bivouac for three days. This included the dreaded 13-mile forced march, which the company was not looking forward to. We had heard horror stories about the march, about recruits falling out due to swollen feet and blood blisters, or collapsing on the ground from exhaustion.

The cattle cars brought us to a clearing in a wooded area. We jumped off and lined up in two single-file formations on both sides of a sand trail. We were loaded to bear, complete 50-pound rucksacks with all of our gear, gas masks at our sides and our rifles. When ordered, we turned right-face. I was in the formation on the right-hand side of the road, behind a burly 19-year-old from Alabama we named "Big Country."

"This ain't so bad," I told myself as we began the march. The drill sergeants were also in full gear, though they lacked the rucksacks. A jeep followed behind at a short distance carrying another drill sergeant.

Four miles into the march, and I began to feel the weight of the rucksack pulling me backwards. I tried in vain to tighten the shoulder straps, but I managed to loosen them instead. This caused me to lean

1. Getting Out of Dodge

forward to try and balance the weight of the rucksack on the center of my back. My body was in an awkward position, trying to balance the rucksack and keep up with Big Country in front of me.

We marched past a soldier who had fallen out, moving himself to the center of the road, but falling behind quickly. I refrained from looking at him, and put my head down. Big Country started pulling away from me, his long Southern legs moving mechanically in giant strides. I fell behind about 15 feet, then forced myself to double time to catch up.

The boots of a hundred recruits kicked up dust from the sandy path, and I could feel the grit on my teeth. I turned to spit, and the normally clear liquid was jet black. I instinctively began to grind my teeth, feeling the sand grains behind crushed between my rear molars. My legs felt like jelly, and finally, we were called to a halt.

"Fifteen minutes, girls!" The two formations collapsed to the ground

The author as a young recruit at Fort, Dix, New Jersey, 1989.

on their respective sides of the road. Just as we were trained, we left the road and collapsed on the ground five feet into the woods. I took my full canteen and emptied half of the contents down my throat, trying to wash away the sandy grit in my mouth. Big Country yelled to me, "You all right, Woody?" He laughed as I groaned. I was too tired to respond, so I just nodded my head. He smiled at me, and I saw only black grime where is teeth ought to be.

"On your feet!" The call of the drill sergeant caused me to jump up and get into formation. A hundred boots shuffled in the sand to their positions.

"Route-step, march!" yelled the drill sergeant, and we began the march again.

My feet were burning, and I felt something wet on my big toe. I knew a blister had popped, but there was no stopping to check it out.

I tried to take my mind off of the march and pictured myself a Confederate soldier force marching toward Fredericksburg. When that didn't work, I tried to recite all of the state capitals, then finally an astronaut walking across the red sand dunes of Mars. I watched as another four soldiers fell out, then realized I was falling behind Big Country again. I picked up the pace and caught up with him, my back straining from my rucksack, and from being hunched over trying to balance it.

We stopped again four miles up the road. I drained my canteen this time and spit the New Jersey sand back to the ground where it belonged. Soldiers passed us in the other direction, looks of desperation on their faces as they fell back to the rear of the formations. I was determined not to be one of those soldiers, and when we were called back into formation, I had found my second wind. We marched the remaining five miles to finally fall to the ground in a great, open field.

I was paired with my bunkmate, and we set up our shelter halves, which is a fancy military term for pup tent. After setting up our tent, we formed up for chow, which were MREs passed out by the drill sergeants. I got the pork and rice in barbecue sauce, while my bunk mate ended up with the tuna and noodles. He made a face at his food, and then asked me to trade.

"C'mon Woody. I'll trade with you next time, I promise."

I laughed at him. "No way, dude. Ain't happening." He shifted on the ground, angry but hungry enough to eat the tuna.

After chow, we were told to dig two-man foxholes. We dug with

1. Getting Out of Dodge

our entrenching tools, and soon we had a five-foot foxhole. At the bottom of the foxhole we dug a grenade sump, a hole at the bottom in the front wall. If an enemy threw a grenade into the foxhole, the soldier could push it into the grenade sump to lessen the chance of injury.

That night, we were called by an alarm out of our tents. We grabbed our gear and jumped into the foxhole. Seconds later, a flare shot into the night sky. It hung in the air, slowly floating down, illuminating the forest. We began to fire our rifles into the dark, the blanks making "pop-pop-pop" sounds in the night.

"Gas, gas, gas!" someone yelled. We rushed to get our masks on and continued firing until the blanks were expended.

I found this part of the training very exciting. It felt real, and emotions were high as we fired into the dark. We ended up sleeping in our foxholes in the event another alarm was called.

The next day we were sent to the much-feared "gas chamber." We went ten at a time into a small, windowless building. We were told to wear our gas masks when we entered, and after everyone was in, the door was closed. The room was filled with smoke, and I could barely see with the mask on. A masked drill sergeant stood in the center of the room and told us to remove our gas masks. We all removed them quickly. I tried to hold my breath, because I knew the room was filled with CS, or tear gas. When I could no longer hold it, I breathed deeply. The first sensation of being gassed was fear; I could not get a lungful of oxygen. My eyes began to tear up, and mucus began to pour from my nose. After trying to breathe in a few times, I doubled over and tried to vomit. I was dry heaving, and I was certain I was going to die in some small building in the middle of New Jersey. Just when I thought all was lost, the door flew open, and we ran outside. We all were flapping our arms like birds to air our uniforms as we ran toward the water station. There, we washed as much of the CS gas from our skin as possible, scrubbing at our eyes and noses. Then and there I decided that if I was ever in the middle of a gas attack, I would have that mask on faster than anyone the Army had ever trained.

To practice hand to hand combat, we fixed bayonets to our rifles and charged at sandbags hung on poles. We screamed at the top of our lungs as we thrust the bayonet through the sandbag, pretending it was an enemy soldier.

Another part of hand to hand combat training was pugil fighting.

Last of the Glow Worms

In the camp, a ring was formed in the grass, where two combatants were fitted with football helmets, given poles with padded ends, and had to use them as weapons, trying to knock the other soldier to the ground.

I was excited for this part of the training. I had read so many Conan the Barbarian and Japanese samurai stories that I believed that I was a weapons expert. When my turn came, I eagerly donned my helmet and was handed a pugil stick, which I greedily ripped from the hands of the soldier who gave it to me.

My opponent stood at the other side of the circle. He was about my height, but he had a little more muscle mass to his frame. We approached each other and tapped sticks. I then took a position I learned from a samurai movie, holding the pugil stick like a bo staff, and crouching, left leg in front. My opponent ran at me, and with a swing of his stick, I was laid out on my back. The crowd hooted and clapped, and I lay there motionless, embarrassed at my five-second performance.

The rest of White Phase proved more mundane. It consisted of the obstacle course and map reading. Shooting an azimuth was a weak point for me, and I needed to keep at it so I could perform well at the soldier stakes, which was the final test for recruits during Blue Phase.

Blue Phase was the last two weeks of basic training. The drill sergeants still yelled and screamed, but with less frequency. The company was on edge for the upcoming soldier stakes. We trained in the final week for the test, going over claymore mines, the LAW (Light Artillery Weapon), and the live hand grenade course.

I was gung-ho about firing the LAW. When my turn came to fire it, I was amazed by how light the weapon was. I extended the weapon, and another soldier loaded it. I raised the forward sights and aimed at a target 150 meters out.

"Backblast area clear!" I yelled, exactly as I was trained. I squeeze the trigger, and a small, slow moving trainer rocket shot out, falling 25 meters short of the target, exploding with blue powder. I at once was disappointed; I thought I was going to fire a live round.

Next came the grenade assault course. We were going to be timed assaulting ground targets with practice grenades. I waited in position, tightening the straps on my Kevlar, and loading my rifle with a 20-round magazine of blanks. The drill sergeant had a stopwatch in his hand and waited for the minute hand to reach 12.

1. Getting Out of Dodge

"Go!" he shouted. I ran down a path into the woods, holding my rifle like I was running a combat mission in Vietnam. I scanned the ground until I saw my first target. I fell to the ground, and the shock caused me to fire a blank round. I forgot our training, which was never to run with your finger on the trigger. Forgetting this mistake, I pulled a hand grenade from my belt and shoved it into a hole in a small bunker. I then rolled to my left and got into a prone firing position until the grenade "popped." I jumped up, ran to the next target, and repeated the same steps, this time remembering to take my finger from the trigger. After the third target was assaulted, I sprinted toward the finish line. The drill sergeant on the opposite end of the course clicked the stopwatch.

"Time!" he yelled, meaning I passed the course.

A final test in soldier stakes was the throwing of two live hand grenades. The grenade range was one of the most nerve-racking experiences I had ever had until that point in the Army. I was on edge as we stood in line, never having been near something as powerful as a hand grenade. The drill sergeants were making light of the situation, keeping morale high by telling offhand jokes and raunchy stories.

When my turn came, I took my spot at grenade station, which was a three-sided, four-foot-high concrete wall. The range itself was about 30 meters long and 15 meters wide. The drill sergeant handed me a grenade, told me to pull the pin, and throw it. I aimed at the old jeep that was out in the middle of the range and threw the grenade like a baseball, ducking quickly behind the wall. The explosion is not like you see on television or in the movies; there was no fireball, just a quick explosion and dust rising from the shrapnel that hit it in a 15-meter radius. I felt the ground shake from the explosion, and it was like nothing I had ever experienced before. We stood up after "All clear!" was shouted, and I was handed my second grenade. I pulled the pin, and this time held onto the grenade for an extra second while trying to aim at the jeep.

"Throw the damn thing!" The drill sergeant's voice rattled me, and I threw the grenade. After the explosion and "All clear!" we stood back up.

I missed the jeep for the second time.

It was our last week before graduation. The Soldiers Stakes test went very well, though I still had problems using a compass to find an azimuth. I was not in a combat MOS, so I brushed it off. I had no plans to be lost in a desert or jungle out in the middle of nowhere.

The last week of basic included a night fire exercise. We were marched to a training course which was covered with low-lying barbed wire and had a large tower on the side. We lined up in full gear at the beginning of the course and a flare was shot into the air. The first recruits fell to the ground and began to low crawl under the barbed wire while a machine gun fired over their heads. When my turn came, I hit the ground and began my low crawl. The bullets flew over my head, and I felt as if I was in real war, low crawling under enemy gunfire. It was an intense night, one that will be forever etched in my memory.

The following day we were issued our Army dress green uniforms, or "Class As." We were also given our weapons qualifications badges to pin onto our Class As. Mine were the sharpshooter badge for the M16 and the grenade badge. I truly felt like a soldier, thinking of the images I had seen of World War II veterans covered in medals, hoping that one day I could also be as decorated as those brave men.

The barracks were more relaxed, though we still had to perform security detail. Our civilian clothes were in a closet in our two-man room, and my roommate discovered that by jiggling the door handle, he could get the door to open. He started digging through his personal belongings, putting on a civilian cardigan sweater and walking down the hall to show off. I stayed in my bunk, dreaming of graduating from basic training.

The whole company was preparing for graduation, everyone excited about going to AIT (advanced individual training) at their respective posts. I knew I would be heading to Redstone Arsenal, Alabama, for AIT, and the other two 55Gs in my company would be going there also. I also knew that I would probably never see any of the soldiers in my company again.

That was a fact of military life. You make friends, and you promise each other you'll meet again, but you know deep down inside that you never will.

We graduated on September 28, 1989, from basic training. Our training unit, Company B, 1st Battalion, 26th Infantry Regiment, stood proudly at attention on the parade grounds. In front of the grandstand, in front of our families and friends, we reaffirmed our oath of allegiance to the United States and to the United States Army. Awards were presented to some soldiers, and those that had college credits were promoted to private E2. We were awarded our Army Service Ribbons and began to march past the grandstand as the band played the Army Song. From that point on, we were officially soldiers.

I was still 17 years old, but I truly felt like a man.

2

Learning the Power of the Atom

There were hundreds of recent basic training graduates at the airport in Newark waiting for their flights to take them to AIT. I was at the American Airlines terminal with Branson and Ulzick, the two other nuke techs who graduated basic with me. We were waiting for a flight to Atlanta with a connecting flight that would take us to Huntsville, Alabama.

The flight to Atlanta went smoothly, but I was horrified by the connecting flight. We boarded a small, twin-engine prop plane. There were only five people on board, an older couple, the two nuke techs, and me. The couple sat near the cockpit, and we three soldiers took seats in the rear. We strapped ourselves in and the plane departed for our two-hour flight to Huntsville. During the flight, the plane rocked and shook, and I tightened my grip on the armrests of my seat. The flight attendant must have noticed as she approached me and asked if I would like something to drink. I asked for a beer, and she hesitated for a moment, then took a beer out of a small cooler in the rear of the plane and gave it to me with a smile. Branson and Ulzick saw this and promptly asked for beer too. When we popped the tabs on the cans, we toasted each other to our success. We were all under 21 years of age, and I was the youngest at 17. Another advantage of wearing the uniform.

Redstone Arsenal is the home of the United States Army Missile and Munitions Center and School, a sprawling Army base about eight square miles in area. After World War II, a number of German scientists and engineers were brought to Redstone Arsenal and contracted to work on the Army's missile program under Operation *Paperclip*. The

2. Learning the Power of the Atom

scientists helped the U.S. Army develop such missile systems as the Honest John, Nike Hercules and Hawk surface-to-surface missiles (the Hawk later became a surface-to-air missile).

Redstone Arsenal's school was used to train soldiers with MOS designators in munitions and missile-related systems.

We were driven to our barracks, which looked like condominiums from the outside. They were light brown, recently constructed. I was impressed at the cleanliness of the buildings, and when we entered, we saw the interior was carpeted, with a main desk at the entrance. There were two floors and I was escorted to the second floor while Ulzick and Branson stayed on the first floor. I was walked to a room where my escort knocked on the door. A few moments later, a young man answered. He was told I was his new roommate. He looked at me, nodded, and opened the door. My escort handed me a key and said to put my gear away in the wall locker. He also said a drill sergeant would summon me shortly. He turned and left, and I went further into the room.

It was a small, two-man room with separate bunks. There was a large window overlooking the front of the building, through which we could see the mess hall. An adjoining washroom, which was very clean, connected our room with our neighbors' room. I could not get over how different AIT living quarters were compared to basic training.

My new roommate snapped me from my daydream. His name was Miggs, and he was from South Carolina. He was a 55B, or an ammunition handler. We shook hands, and I knew then and there that this was going to work out. I began to load my wall locker, taking my rolled-up tee-shirts and BDUs out of my duffle bag, unrolling them and hanging them up in the locker. I just got to padlocking the locker when there was a knock on the door. I answered and was summoned to the drill sergeant's office just down the hall. I followed my escort and noticed people hanging around the information desk near the stairs. There were men and women there, and I quickly realized the barracks were co-ed. Yes, this definitely was going to be good.

The drill sergeant welcomed me into his office with a handshake and a smile. He asked me to be seated and began to pore over some papers on his desk. He started by telling me he was one of my instructors, and his name was Staff Sergeant Hernandez. He was also a 55G and had been stationed at Fort Carson, Colorado. and Fort Drum, New York. He had spent a tour in South Korea and Turkey. He would be one of our instructors on weapons systems maintenance, along with two other drill sergeants. We would also have an instructor for basic electronics and introduction to radiation testing equipment. All of the instructors would be fellow 55Gs. Staff Sergeant Hernandez continued by saying that I should be very proud for entering this MOS, as there were only 500 or so nuke techs in the entire Army. Everyone knows everyone, and they take care of each other.

His speech put me at ease, and I started to relax. I also experienced speaking to an NCO and not saying "sergeant" before or after every sentence, which felt strange at first; it was hard to break the habit once you were in it, as my exchanges demonstrated, and it was also a matter of respect. We began to speak about our personal lives, and he asked me where I was going to permanent station. I told him Germany, but I did not know where yet. He said that as soon as I find out to let him know, and he would call ahead to give me a nice introduction. After chatting for a few more minutes, Staff Sergeant Hernandez got down to business.

"The training will be mentally challenging. After PT and chow, we begin promptly at 9 a.m. Monday through Thursday will be weapons training, Fridays will be electronics training. You will need to pass an end of AIT exam and also a PT test before you are allowed to graduate.

"In addition, I will be inspecting your quarters once a week. I expect your living area to be spotless. You are confined to the Arsenal for your first week. After that, you are free to come and go as you please, as long as you are back in your quarters by 10 p.m. on weekdays. You have no curfew on Friday and Saturday nights. Do you understand?"

"Yes, sergeant," I replied.

"Any questions?"

"No, sergeant. I'm good."

"Okay, you can return to your quarters. Good night."

"Good night, sergeant," I replied. I stood and took his hand. He smiled at me, and I left his office for my room. As I walked down the hallway, I noticed Ulzick hanging out at the information desk with a group of people. I looked the two girls over that were standing there with Ulzick then turned and nodded my head at the guys.

"They're all 55Gs," started Ulzick. "We'll be in class together." He grinned, which caused me to crack a smile. I introduced myself, and we stood around, talking about our experiences in basic training and where we would be stationed after AIT. Honestly, we all hit it off pretty well. I guess Staff Sergeant Hernandez was right.

Nuke techs take care of each other.

The following Monday we began weapons training. There were four nuclear weapons systems that we were trained on: the MGM-52 Lance and Pershing II missile systems and the M454 (155-mm) and the M422 (eight-inch) nuclear projectiles.

The Lance Missile System

The Lance missile system was a tactical surface-to-surface ballistic missile that was designed to carry either a nuclear warhead (W-70 designation) or an HE (high explosive) warhead. The range of the missile was between 45 and 75 miles, depending on which warhead was installed. They were fired from M752 missile launchers, with two launchers and two M688 transport vehicles completing a Lance battery. They had a fire rate of three missiles an hour.

There were more than 2000 Lance missiles produced with eight battalions fielding them: six battalions in European countries including Germany, Italy, Britain, the Netherlands and Belgium, and two battalions in the United States. The U.S. Army was the custodian of the nuclear warheads in Europe; in case of a Soviet invasion, the warheads would be released to their host country's military for use in battle.

There was also a modification to the W-70 warhead, named W-70MOD3. The MOD3 was an enhanced radiation nuclear warhead, or "neutron bomb," which, when exploded, had a smaller blast area, but dispersed high levels of radiation over a larger area. This was to cause minimal damage to infrastructure, such as buildings and roads, and maximum radiation kills to enemy soldiers.

The Pershing II Missile System

The Pershing II missile was an intermediate-range guided ballistic missile with a range of 1100 miles. The complete missile system weighed more than 16,000 pounds and included a radar section, warhead, guidance section, and first and second rocket boosters.

The missile was transported using the M983 HEMTT (Heavy Expanded Mobility Tactical Truck) to missile batteries, which would fire the missile from the M1003 launcher. It was fitted with the W85 nuclear warhead, which was a variable yield warhead that could be set for an explosion between five and 80 kilotons of TNT. There were 108 Pershing II tactical nuclear missiles deployed in Europe, all in West Germany.

The deployment of the weapons system was controversial. Protests were carried out against the Pershing II throughout western Europe in 1983, with an estimated 500,000 people forming a human chain from the U.S. Army Headquarters in Stuttgart, West Germany, to the gates of Wiley Barracks in Neu-Ulm, where a Pershing missile battalion was stationed. The deployment of the Pershing II was in direct response to the Soviet deployment of SS-20 Saber intermediate-range nuclear missiles, which had a range of more than 3300 miles and were deployed in Siberia.

The M454 Nuclear Projectile

The M454 was an artillery-fired, air burst nuclear projectile weighing around 130 pounds. It was fired from the M114 or M109 howitzers and had a range between nine and 15 miles. The M454 consisted of the W48 nuclear warhead, which is an implosion-type fission weapon, and had an explosive yield of approximately 72 tons of TNT, which is relatively low compared to other nuclear artillery and nuclear ballistic missiles. A dial-a-yield device was also installed, which allowed the operating battery to select the explosive power of the weapon. As with the M422 projectile, the M454 was secured with a PAL (permissive action link), which was a combination lock attached to the nose-cone of the shell.

The system was deployed in Europe in West Germany, Italy, Greece and Turkey. In Asia, it was deployed in South Korea.

The M422 Nuclear Projectile

The M422CA1E1 was an artillery-fired nuclear projectile which began production in 1957. It weighed 200 pounds and was 44 inches in length, and it consisted of the W79 nuclear warhead. The W79 was a linear implosion, fission-type nuclear weapon with a yield between 0.8 and 1.1 kilotons of TNT. Two modifications were made to the W79: MOD0 was variable yield and also had an enhanced radiation selection; MOD1 was a straight fission weapon with no variable yield option. The M422 was fitted with a PAL system, which consisted of a combination lock which was fitted over the breechblock fuse at the base of the weapon.

The projectile was fired from the M110 or M115 howitzer and had a range of just under 10 miles. This weapon system was deployed in West Germany, Italy, Greece, Turkey and South Korea.

Our class consisted of 20 soldiers, an almost equal mix of males and females. We trained first with the missile systems, and I listened intently as the instructors explained how the systems worked and what needed to be done to keep them in top condition. We practiced repairing the ablative material on the trainer Lance and Pershing II warheads. The material was a soft, cork-like substance that would absorb heat on the vehicle's body upon reentry into the atmosphere. The material was in a thick liquid form stored in small aluminum cans and would harden after exposure to oxygen.

The warheads were stored in olive-drab containers with the standard U.S. Army markings on the outside designating which system was stored within. We would use a stencil machine to punch out cardboard letters and numbers, retouch the paint on the outside of the container and use the stencils with black spray paint to identify the weapon system on the outside of the container.

For the Lance and Pershing IIs, we also checked the thermal batteries within the warheads and removed or repaired battery gaskets.

Friday would come and we would attend our electronics class. We had a separate instructor, who was also a 55G, for this class. I took an interest in this part of the training and listened attentively as she spoke. We went over basic circuitry, the fundamentals of electricity, and how to use various test equipment, like ohmmeters, oscillators and multimeters. The test equipment would be used to calibrate the various radiac meters, or Geiger counters, we would be using during maintenance of the weapons systems. The training room was very large, and the instructor guided on us on the use of each piece of equipment. She was very easygoing and knowledgeable about the duties we were going to be performing.

She was a sergeant, but we called her by her first name, and I was starting to see a pattern among nuke techs. I was 100 percent sure that an infantryman in AIT would not be calling his instructors by their first names, and I'm sure if he did, he would be feeling the wrath of the drill sergeant rain down upon him in the form of the front leaning rest position.

Just then, I thought of the 11C who was in our basic training unit. He was probably at Fort Benning cleaning toilets with a toothbrush at this very moment.

I had never been this far south before, and Huntsville, Alabama, felt very different from Chicago. The people moved slower; driving, eating, talking, they took their time, like there was no hurry to get anywhere to do anything. They were noticeably more friendly here than up north, and most went out of their way to help a stranger.

On our second weekend, we were allowed off the arsenal for the day. I went with Ulzick to the U.S. Space and Rocket Museum in Huntsville. We had to wear our Class A uniforms, which was fine with me, but bugged the heck out of Ulzick. I really enjoyed going out in public in my dress uniform—the looks we got from civilians, especially the girls! We finished dressing, and I brought out a new round Army cap that I bought at the PX, the type with the black bill and front and the gold Army insignia on the face. Officers wore these caps often, and they were also available to enlisted soldiers, minus the gold leaves lining both sides of the black bill. Ulzick shook his head, putting on his Army-issue garrison cap.

The Space and Rocket Museum was a welcomed getaway from life at Redstone. We toured the moon landing exhibit and stood in awe of the Saturn V Rocket, which sent astronauts to the moon. We walked around slowly, taking everything in, and I tried to compare what we were seeing to what we were going to be doing when we finished AIT. Rockets were an integral part of our MOS, and I wanted to get a basic understanding of the physics behind them. Ulzick was also interested in rocketry and was also more scientifically inclined than I was. After our tour of the museum, we asked one of the older soldiers to buy us a six-pack of beer. Alcohol was not allowed in the barracks, so we stood behind the PX in the rain and drank them, smoking cigarettes and laughing about nothing. I knew my time with Ulzick was limited; I would be heading to Germany after AIT, and he was going to Fort Carson,

2. Learning the Power of the Atom

Colorado. Feeling tipsy, we walked back to the barracks and went to our quarters. Lying in bed, I began thinking whether or not I would see any of these other nuke techs again.

The following Monday we had a special training event. Our platoon was driven to an isolated area of the arsenal, which was a small grove surrounded by trees. There was a concrete bunker on the edge of the grove, and ten seven-foot-high poles lined up about ten meters in front of it. We got out of the truck and met members of the Army's EOD (explosive ordnance disposal) soldiers. Staff Sergeant Hernandez shook hands with one of them, and we were ordered into formation. Today, we were going to train with C4, or plastic explosives. I suddenly became super excited; as kids, my friends and I would play war, and we were always trying to find new ways of throwing pretend plastic explosives at each other. Rambo used it, Arnold used it. We even tried to be hip and call it *plastique*, just as the French would.

The reason for training with C4 was explained to us; at our permanent stations, there would be security protocols we would have to train for, which included shape charges (cone-shaped containers of C4), which would be placed over the nuke containers, wired with det (detonating) cord, and exploded. This would be in the event of an imminent loss of nuclear weapons, either by the Soviets or Warsaw Pact (if in Europe), China or North Korea (if in Asia), or domestic terrorists in the United States.

The EOD specialists showed us how to thread the det cord through holes at the six-foot mark on the poles. Smaller pieces of the cord were then wrapped around the main line at eight-foot intervals and allowed to hang down. These smaller pieces were then fitted with blasting caps. After we fitted the blasting caps, EOD formed small balls of C4 and fitted them over the caps. When the setup was finished, it looked like a long clothesline with baseballs hanging down, rocking back and forth in a light wind. We were then directed to the bunker as an EOD specialist unwound the det cord from the spool and led it into the bunker. We were packed in tight, and the end of the det cord was cut and an igniter was fitted over the end. The igniter was a small, cylinder-shaped device with a pull ring on the end. EOD asked for a volunteer to pull the ring. Naturally, everyone raised their hands. They picked Nathans, one of only three females in our platoon.

Nathans held the igniter tight in her left hand, and put the index finger of her right hand through the ring. We all squeezed together to watch out of the blast-resistant glass on the bunker. As we waited, two birds flew into the grove and landed on the cord. I wanted to yell "Wait!" but EOD gave the order to fire at the exact same moment. Nathans pulled the ring and almost instantaneously the balls of C4 exploded. Everyone cheered, myself included. We laughed and slapped each other on the backs, and then I thought of the birds. They were vaporized in an instant, and I thought about that as we drove back to the arsenal. They were just birds, destroyed by weapons meant for humans.

In November, an F4 tornado hit the southern portion of Huntsville. Though we were not in the tornado's path, a part of our barracks' roof was ripped off of the building. There were no injuries, and life continued as normal as the roof was repaired.

November was also the first time I saw snow in Alabama, and judging by the closing of the arsenal, it was the first time for many Alabamians. It was only an inch of snow, but people were in a panic. Cars drove a steady five miles per hour while others ended up sliding off of the road that ran through the arsenal. It was surreal; if they panicked at a dusting of snow, they would have died of heart attacks if they lived in Chicago.

At the end of November, we went on bivouac for a couple of days. It was the entire training company, and we lugged our gear out to the field, only to end up staying in large, 20-man tents, which were split by platoons. The temperature that night got down to 15 degrees, which was a record for the Huntsville area. I rolled my sleeping pad on the ground, then put my sleeping bag over it, before I slid in. I zipped up the bag and removed my clothing, stripping down to my t-shirt and underwear. The purpose of stripping was to let your body heat warm you inside of the sleeping bag. 11Bs were doing drills like this constantly, and I gained a new respect for them, having to endure the elements so regularly.

I walked with Ulzick to the mess hall for morning chow and noticed a crowd of soldiers forming a circle around someone. Curious, I pressed in closer, and realized the soldier standing in the middle of the crowd wore a green beret.

There is only one group of soldiers authorized to wear green berets, and those are Special Forces. I moved in closer, just as curious as everyone else. He was tall, and he wore jump boots that were unpolished.

2. Learning the Power of the Atom

Sergeant stripes were sewn on his sleeve, and he seemed to be in the middle of telling a story to the crowd of admirers. They laughed when he laughed, and cooed when he cooed. It was painful to watch, but I could understand the fascination. I don't know why he was here, and the only explanation I could think of was that he was reclassifying to a new specialty.

Losing interest, we continued our trek to the mess hall.

The following weekend, we rented a room at the Knights Inn. There were five of us, and we had one of the older soldiers buy the beer, and we celebrated nothing in particular. There were a few of the female 55Gs present, but we looked at them more as buddies than available companions. We toasted each other and told stories about our hometowns, which I quickly realized was a favorite pastime in the military. We spoke of our training and of the drill sergeants we liked or disliked. We also talked of our new duty stations, where we would be leaving for in just over a month. I learned that only two of us would be heading for Europe, while the rest were staying CONUS.

I took photos of the people in room, catching them smiling, yawning, laughing and eventually passed out sleeping. I knew that the chances of me seeing them again were very slim, and I wanted to capture the moment forever.

I learned that a strip club was also on the arsenal and was asked if I wanted to go. It was Ulzick, Branson, and some other guys from down the hall who wanted to check it out. I had just turned 18 and decided to join them.

The club was small and dark, filled with cigarette smoke and the smell of spilled whiskey. There was a bar along one wall and folding chairs encircling a round stage. We sat in the back and watched as the girl came to the stage. The music began and she started her show. There was much to be desired, to say the least. I could instantly tell that she was hesitant about her current job, and her limbs were stiff as she tried to dance provocatively to the music. The audience was yelling and cheering, egging her on to "Take it off!" I sat there watching her, then turned to watch Ulzick and Branson as they sucked down whiskey sours. Everyone was getting wild and drunk, and I sat there sober, since I was still underage. I began to lose interest in the scene altogether, so I got up and walked back to the barracks. There, I hung around the main desk with some other soldiers before deciding to call my father.

Christmas was in a couple of weeks, and I had not seen my family since basic training. My father answered the phone, we talked for a while, and he told me he would drive down and pick me up for Christmas. We were going to be given a two-week leave for the holidays, so I agreed.

The nine-hour drive from Huntsville to Chicago went quickly. My father was not a talker, but we passed the time telling our various experiences with the military. The Vietnam era was a tougher time for soldiers, and drill sergeants were given more leeway in disciplining misconduct, or "perceived" misconduct. He was amazed when I told him our barracks were co-ed and had carpeting and quarters with private bathrooms. He related sleeping in a one-room barrack with 100 other soldiers, all piled together on bunk beds and sharing one latrine. I was sure that combat arms MOSs were probably still experiencing this type of housing. We were different, though, I told him. We were glow worms.

I was invited to a party as soon as I got back to Chicago. It was given by a friend of mine who ended up in jail as soon as we got out of high school. His claim to fame was selling stolen clothes from the trunk of his car. He served a few months in the Cook County Jail and was released on house arrest. He decided to throw himself a "getting out party," and when I arrived, the house was packed with people I either hung around with in high school or had little contact with. He told everyone I was in the Army, and girls would come up to me and ask me questions, showing more than a passing interest that I was a soldier.

One in particular, who never looked at me twice in high school, asked if I remembered her. She was a pretty blonde, short, and rather drunk at this point.

"No, I don't remember you," I replied, lying to her. She just smiled and walked away and I resumed drinking. A couple of hours into the party, the police showed up. We were taken down to the station for underage drinking. While the other partygoers were scrambling to call parents or friends to pick them up, my situation was different. When the police found out I was enlisted, they asked me where the nearest MP station was.

"Fort Sheridan in Lake Forest," I responded, still quite tipsy. The cop told me to wait, and he disappeared into an office with a plainclothes

2. Learning the Power of the Atom

officer. They returned a short time later and released me. The plainclothes officer winked at me as I left the holding room, and I realized that being in the military had its perks in the civilian world too.

After New Year's Day, I packed my duffle bag and said goodbye to my family. Graduation was in a week, and I would be leaving for Germany immediately afterwards.

Before graduation, we had to take a PT test, hands-on and final written exam. I held the feet of one of the female nuke techs as she did her sit-ups, counting, "1, 2, 3..." They had to pass with 30 sit-ups, and she stopped at 25, completely drained of strength. I wrote 31 on her card, and she hugged me in appreciation. I could not bring myself to fail a woman who tried hard and was also a nuke tech like myself.

The hands-on exam was fairly simple, and if we made a mistake, the drill sergeant would correct us, and have us repeat the section. I could see that no one would fail this part of the test.

The written exam was just as simple; we were allowed to use notes, though not everyone did, preferring to try to "wing it" from memory, and the questions were all multiple choice. At the end of the exam, the drill sergeant graded the tests, and no one failed.

The graduation ceremony was small, and we received our graduation certificate for 55G: Nuclear Weapons Technician and a certificate showing our affiliation in the Army Ordnance Corps. We partied after the ceremony, and Staff Sergeant Hernandez handed me my orders. I was going to be stationed at the 64th Ordnance Company in Fischbach, West Germany. He knew a warrant officer who happened to be stationed there at the moment and said he would contact him to let him know I was coming there. I thanked him, and he then told me a secret.

There were two female soldiers who had been giving the instructors a hard time. They were troublemakers, he said, and anonymously reported the instructors were being harder on them than the other 55Gs in the platoon. Staff Sergeant Hernandez knew this because he had disciplined them numerous times for not keeping their quarters clean to Army standards. He knew that both were going to be stationed at Fort Drum in New York, and he also made a phone call to promptly announce their upcoming arrival, but not in a good way.

Ulzik, I learned, was going to Fort Carson, Colorado. Branson was going to South Korea. I was the only one from my platoon going to the 64th; there was another soldier named Klemberg heading to the 619th Ordnance Company in Kriegsfeld, West Germany.

On my last night In Huntsville, I stayed at a hotel to wait for the morning flight to Atlanta. After getting something to eat, I watched TV, flicking through the channels, not really watching anything, and not paying to attention to the programs I was flipping through.

There was a soft knock at my door, and I opened it to find one of the girls I had graduated from AIT with standing there with a big smile. She was very short, just barely touching five feet, but she had a big personality. I remembered talking to her during training on the Lance system, and she was very friendly, asking me personal questions about where I was from and how I liked the military.

I invited her into the room, and she sat down in the soft easy chair next to the desk in the corner. We made small talk, mostly about our fear and excitement at going to new stations. She was being stationed stateside, at Fort Lewis, Washington.

After we had been talking for a few minutes, there was another knock at the door. She got up to answer it, while I sat back on the bed, still flipping through channels. One of our drill sergeants from AIT entered the room and took a seat in the easy chair. She walked over to him and sat on his lap. They gave each other a kiss on the lips, which made me turn my head.

During one of our talks before graduation, the girl had asked me if they could rendezvous in my room that night. I told her it was no problem, just come on by. She trusted me, as did the drill sergeant, with keeping their affair a secret. I had suspected their relationship but had never made it point to pursue the truth. It wasn't my business, and I tended to stay out of people's personal affairs.

They sat with me and chatted for a bit before leaving the hotel room. The drill sergeant shook my hand and wished me luck as a new 55G. The girl leaned in and hugged me. I wished them all the best and watched them leave together, arm-in-arm.

I was sure fraternization happened in the military, but this was the first time I had ever witnessed it. It was also the first time that I was charged with holding such a big secret.

The next morning, I caught a prop plane from Huntsville to Atlanta. From there, I flew to Frankfurt, Germany. The flight seemed to take

2. Learning the Power of the Atom

forever, but I refrained from drinking alcohol on the plane to pass the time. It was a civilian flight, and there were a few uniformed soldiers, each wearing their Class As. I was too excited to sleep, but my eyes became heavy when we got over the Atlantic. I was soon dreaming about a new experience in Europe.

3

Wilkommen in Deutschland

I stood at the end of the airplane's exit ramp, closed my eyes, and took a deep breath.

Germany. I was finally here.

I entered the terminal at Frankfurt's Rhein-Main International Airport, where I walked with a group of newly-arrived soldiers to the welcome center. I noticed the differences between American and European airports instantly. Security is performed by German police in green uniforms carrying machine guns. The terminal is filled with people from every corner of the earth, Arabs, Asians, Africans, Europeans and Americans, speaking a myriad of languages, trying to get to their departure concourses.

There were airport stores, called kiosks, that sold everything from magazines to souvenirs to alcohol. The random American soldier rushed by, duffle bag over his shoulder in the fireman's carry, trying to catch a plane back to the States. The airport in Frankfurt also houses a USO office for American soldiers who need a safe place to go while waiting for their flights.

I was dressed in my Class A uniform, the Army Service Medal the solitary ribbon on my chest. I quickly learned that the noobs, the soldiers being deployed to Germany for the first time, were the only ones wearing their Class As. I followed the herd of soldiers, and we were guided to a bus which took us to the processing station for new arrivals. Processing took place at the 21st Replacement Battalion in Frankfurt. We would be staying there for a three-day orientation before we were shipped out to our duty stations. I was fortunate in meeting a staff sergeant who was going to the 64th with me and who just happened to also be a nuke tech. Staff Sergeant Washington was in his late 30s and had been stationed in Germany before but at a different nuke site. This would be his first time stationed in Fischbach, but he mentioned he knew a few of the NCOs who were stationed there and were also preparing for his arrival.

We began in-processing the next morning. I filled out paperwork to set up a bank account that would be located at the main bank in the Husterhoeh Kaserne in Pirmasens, which was the headquarters for the 197th Ordnance Battalion and 27 kilometers north of Fischbach. After the necessary paperwork, we began a course in the German language called "Headstart." This program went over basic phrases in German, the culture, and the relationship between LNs (local nationals) and the American military. I had taken German for three years in high school and had an understanding of the language. I could hold a conversation in German, albeit at an elementary level.

The next training phase consisted of the Warsaw Pact in general and the Soviet Union in particular. We were to be on the lookout for SMLM (Soviet Military Liaison Mission) vehicles. The SMLM were Soviet intelligence personnel who were allowed to travel throughout West Germany to observe whether offensive measures were underway in NATO against the Warsaw Pact. The United States, Great Britain and France had intelligence personnel in East Germany for the same purpose. According to the Huebner-Malinin Agreement, these intelligence units were allowed to travel freely in their respective AORs (area of responsibility), but were prohibited from approaching or gathering information in the vicinity of military bases.

There was one incident which resulted in the death of an American MLM on March 23, 1985. Major Arthur Nicholson was on a mission to photograph a Soviet storage building in Ludwigslust, which was a town located 100 miles north of Berlin. He was discovered by Soviet sergeant Aleksandr Ryabstev, who opened fire on Major Nicholson and his driver, Sergeant Schatz. The major was struck by gunfire and killed, the last casualty of the MLM intelligence missions of the Cold War in Germany.

The three-day orientation went by quickly, after which we boarded a bus for Pirmasens. During the ride, I was amazed at how clean Germany was and how efficient the roadways were. Passing was not permitted in the right lane, and traffic in the left lane had to drive faster than the right lane. I watched as beautiful Mercedes sedans passed the bus at speeds of more than 100 miles an hour.

As we drove, the flatlands of Hesse started to break up into small hills, which lead to the state of Rhineland-Palatinate and the city of Pirmasens.

Rhineland-Palatinate is a state in West Germany formed from the French protectorate area after World War II.

Historically, the region was inhabited by various Celtic tribes, who were eventually expelled by the Roman empire around 12 BC. The area became part of the Roman province Germania Superior. More powerful Germanic tribes from east of the Rhein River began raiding the weakened Romans during the third century with a coalition of Germanic tribes (Alamanni) eventually settling there.

The Franconians under King Clovis I conquered the territory from the Alamanni in 496, adding it to the Kingdom of the Franks.

The first recording of the name Pirmasens was in 860, as the name Pirminiseusna. The city and surrounding towns have been ruled by many factions throughout their history, the Celts, Romans, Alamanni, Franks, Bavarians and French in addition to many smaller feudal and religious rulers until the 19th century.

With the unification of the German states into one political entity under Otto von Bismarck in January 1871, Rhineland and Palatinate became part of the German empire.

The defeat of the Central Powers in World War I allowed the Allies to dismantle the short-lived German empire; the Germans kept Saarland and Palatinate but lost Alsace and Lorraine.

During his drive into Germany during World War II, Patton and the American Third Army passed through Saarland, with the 71st Infantry Division capturing Pirmasens on March 15, 1945.

Palatinate is covered in thick forests and hills, with towns spread apart and connected by small, winding roads. Rapeseed fields, formed into perfect squares, are cultivated on the sides of cleared hills. Surprisingly well-maintained and partially-ruined castles dot the countryside despite centuries of warfare. Rock formations, carved over millennia from erosion, are popular hiking and rock climbing areas.

The American military established a base over the remains of an abandoned German army base in Pirmasens named Huesterhoeh Kaserne. The *Kaserne* (barracks in German, but also used frequently by Americans) is located on a plateau to the north of the city, with extensive underground tunnels and caves connecting it to nearby

3. Wilkommen in Deutschland

towns. Huesterhoeh Kaserne became the center of the Pirmasens military community, which oversaw military installations in Münchweiler, Clausen, Dahn, Fischbach, Massweiler, and numerous other smaller installations.

Once we arrived, Staff Sergeant Washington and I began our in-processing into the 197th Ordnance Battalion. We were shown to our temporary quarters where we dropped off our luggage. We were then led to the battalion headquarters building, where a woman behind a large, chest-high desk gave us a map of Huesterhoeh Kaserne and the surrounding area. We filled out the paperwork to transfer our driver's licenses to military licenses and received our ration cards. I held the card in my hand, confused. Staff Sergeant Washington took notice and explained.

"You can only purchase so many bottles of whiskey or cartons of cigarettes a year. Each time you buy one or the other, the cashier will fill in one of the small boxes on the card. When the card is filled up, no more booze or cigarette purchases until the year has gone by. Or you can use someone else's card that doesn't smoke or drink. They do that because we do not pay tax on cigarettes and alcohol here."

Our business finished in the welcome center, I went with Staff Sergeant Washington to where the supply building was located. I followed him, due to his experience PCSing to different places and because he was a genuinely nice man. We made our way to the supply building and were issued our gear. I noticed it was the same gear that I was issued in basic and AIT, which was a relief since I was now familiar with it all. We signed for our gear and went to the PX, which was located across the street from the main kaserne.

The PX was larger than those I had seen at Fort Dix or Redstone Arsenal. It was filled wall to wall with every kind of American food and electronic device you could think of. I browsed the goods, walking down every aisle and inspecting as many items as I could. I had some money burning a hole in my pocket, and Washington advised me to purchase a transformer since Europe runs on 220V electricity and our electronics will not plug into their outlets. In addition to the transformer, I picked up a few magazines to keep me occupied until we reached Fischbach. When I got to the checkout line, I was standing behind five other customers, some with shopping carts full of goods. I waited patiently, until I heard a voice and the lady in front of me nudged my arm.

"Come on up," says the cashier, speaking from behind her counter. I looked around. "Me?" I ask her.

"Yes, come on up."

I walked to the front of the line, timid at being singled out.

"New here?" she asked, scanning my transformer.

"Yes, ma'am," I replied. I reached up and scratched the back of my head.

"Uniformed personnel always come to the front of the line." She handed me my bag and receipt. "Have a good day."

Walking back from the PX to the kaserne, I noticed a Burger King on the corner. I talked Washington into going there with me, bribing him with a free lunch. In the parking lot, I saw German cars, which all seemed to be Mercedes or BMWs. Their license plates were larger than ours, and they began with the letters "PS," which stood for Pirmasens. Staff Sergeant Washington explained that German license plates all began with the abbreviation for the county, or *Landkreis*, that the owner of the vehicle lived in. Inside, I stood in line with other soldiers, American civilians, and German nationals who waited to place their orders. I strained to listen to the Germans as they spoke, trying to pick up words here and there. I wanted to be fluent in German to get the full experience of living in the host country.

After our lunch, we headed back to our quarters. I stayed in the rest of the evening, reading *Spin* magazine, waiting for the morning to arrive with the bus that would take us to Fischbach.

The bus ride from Pirmasens to Fischbach was one of the most amazing rides I had ever taken to this point in my life. We wound our way through the hills, which resembled those I had seen in Big Stone Gap, Virginia, in the Appalachian Mountains, where my father was from but these had beautiful, naturally-occurring sandstone formations that dotted the area. We stopped at a small military installation in the town of Münchweiler. We were allowed off the bus and I went to the snack bar to get something to eat. An hour later, we boarded the bus again for Fischbach. We passed through small, picturesque towns that I tried to remember the names of, the first being Hinterweidenthal. There we turned right onto the B427 and after a few miles ended up in Dahn. A small Army detachment was located outside of the town, and the bus stopped and some soldiers got off.

As we wound through the town, my heart almost leaped from my

3. Wilkommen in Deutschland

chest; an old castle, half in ruins, was sitting on top of one of the hills. I stared at it until it disappeared from view, forcing myself to remember the name of the town that it was in, so I could go back and explore it.

We passed through a couple more towns, Bruckweiler and then Bundenthal, where we once again turned right. I saw a sign that read *Fischbach bei Dahn*. We drove through the town, and about two miles further, on a narrow, two-lane road, I saw the barbed wire fence. On my right I saw a motor pool filled with trucks and then a gate straight ahead. The bus drove to the gate and a sign greeted us: *Welcome to the Fischbach Army Depot.*

The Fischbach Army Depot was located one mile southwest of the town of Fischbach bei Dahn and a half-mile west of the small hamlet of Peterbaechel. It sprawled over 1,300 acres of forest and hills, with the southern perimeter of the depot ending at the French border. Though the land area was large, there were only 300 or so soldiers stationed there. Most lived in one of the three co-ed barracks, while those

Welcome to Fischbach sign, 1987 (photograph by and courtesy of Katherine Gallagher).

with families lived in rented homes in nearby towns or at the Bunker Hill family housing buildings in Pirmasens.

The barracks were World War II–style billets, rectangular with three floors and rooms on both sides of a hallway that ran the length of the building. They were white, concrete structures with windows that swung outward in the European style. Window screening was noticeably absent.

A day room was located near the entrance of the barracks and was a kind of gathering place for the soldiers who lived there. A TV was in the room, along with a soda machine that someone thoughtfully filled with Coke, Sprite and Budweiser beer.

A phone was present at the small desk near the entrance and could be used to receive calls from off base.

The 165th Military Police Company were housed in one barracks, while the 64th Ordnance Company was housed in the other. The 165th MP barracks were under construction when I arrived, and temporary housing structures were set up in front of the barracks to house the displaced soldiers until the renovations were complete.

The third barracks building was located down a small hill from the main barracks, next to a basketball court. The 41st Ordnance Detachment was housed there.

The depot included a small PX, a library and an EM (enlisted members) club. A German national ran a barber shop on the depot, and there was also a drycleaner for those who wished to have their uniforms laundered for a fee. A small gym was located just up the hill from the barracks. There was also a building that once housed a theater, but the building was being used for indoor formations.

Across the street from the main gate was a bowling alley, and just to the east was the motor pool.

The area inside the gates was divided into three areas: Area One, Area Two, and the general area.

The general area was located directly through the main gate, which housed the barracks, PX, EM club, and so on. Civilians, both American and German nationals, were allowed in the general area. The headquarters building, where the offices of the company commander and XO (executive officer) and post office were located, were just inside of the main gate.

Only soldiers were allowed to enter Area Two, which had a gate guard. This gate opened deeper into the depot's interior and required a "blue border pass" to be accessed. All soldiers stationed in Fischbach were issued blue border passes. Area Two contained the admin building, which housed the armory and signal equipment and was where staff duty was performed. Further along the road, grass-covered concrete bunkers housed equipment in storage for the three units stationed in Fischbach. The 41st Ordnance Company worked in Area Two, and the Lance and Pershing II missiles first and second stage sections were stored there in bunkers. There was also a training building located on the access road, which was for various uses, including driver's training for deuce-and-a-halfs.

Area One was located deep within the depot and housed the nuclear arsenal, for which the 64th were custodians. This was a NATO secure site, and access was limited to security, the nuke techs, and those who had a duty directly involving the mission being performed there. To enter Area One, a black border pass had to be shown. These passes were issued to nuke techs, the military police performing site security, and other personnel who had duties there.

The perimeter of Area One was enclosed by a double row of seven-foot fences, topped with barbed wire and concertina (razor) wire. The main entrance by vehicle was secured by "tank stoppers," six-foot-long hollow-steel poles inserted at a 45-degree angle into holes in the concrete facing outwards. To enter the site by vehicle, the poles had to be manually pulled from their slots and set to the side. Motion sensors, called volumetrics, were located at intervals along the outside of the area's perimeter. When triggered, they would set off an alarm to the main security building, located at the main entrance to the site. The main security building was a concrete structure with one large watchtower jutting from its side. The watchtower was 30 feet high and also made of concrete. Windows wrapped around the top of the tower, allowing the security detail a 360-degree view of the site and surrounding area.

Inside of the fence, small, one-man watchtowers were placed at intervals along the entire perimeter. The MPs would man the towers, and change at regular shifts, rotating between towers until their shift was complete.

The entire depot was surrounded by hills and forest. It was relatively remote with a bus running a few times a day that went to Pirmasens. Access was limited to a single road, the K43, that winds in front of the

Guard tower at entrance to Area One, 1994 (courtesy Horst Himbacher).

depot, eventually turning north and running into the small town of Ludwigswinkel.

The K43 eventually ran into the L487, called "Thunder Road" by the Americans and the "Edelsteig" by the Germans. Thunder Road was a dangerous, two-lane road that twisted and turned with 90-degree bends, eventually leading to the town of Salzwoog.

A Hawk Missile battery was stationed on Thunder Road just south of Salzwoog. This remote facility was charged with air defense for the Fischbach Army Depot. Like the Fischbach depot, this facility was also remote, completely surrounded by forest. Charlie Battery, 2/56 ADA (Air Defense Artillery) was stationed here, and the bus from Fischbach to Pirmasens would stop here also to pick up or drop off soldiers.

The 64th Ordnance Company

The 64th Ordnance Company entered the regular Army in 1933. It served in six campaigns of World War II, including North Africa and

3. Wilkommen in Deutschland

Germany. After the war, the company was stationed at Adak, Alaska, as the 64th Ordnance Base Depot Company until 1958, when it was redesignated as the 64th Ordnance Company (Special Weapons and Ammo), supporting the U.S. Army Artillery and Missile School.

In 1959, the 64th was deployed to Fischbach, West Germany, part of the 82nd Ordnance Battalion AWSCOM (Advanced Weapons Support Command). In September 1965, the 82nd Ordnance Battalion was deactivated, and the 64th was assigned directly under AWSCOM.

AWSCOM and the Special Ammunition Support Command merged in November 1972, assigning the 64th Ordnance Company to the newly-formed 197th Ordnance Battalion.

The 64th provided DS (direct support) of nuclear weapons to American artillery units in West Germany and was an alternate to the 9th Ordnance Company (Miesau) providing theater support of special weapons.

There were 100 soldiers assigned to the 64th, divided into four platoons. These included the M&A (maintenance and assembly), Alpha Platoon, Bravo Platoon and the HQ (headquarters) Platoon.

In the late 1970s, the 64th Ordnance Company was at half strength. Vehicle operators were trained as ammunition handlers to help with the mission. According to accounts by officers previously stationed in Fischbach, half of the truck trailers were missing. They had to scour the forest to find them and discovered some on logging trails and still others in between trees. After a new motor pool officer was assigned to Fischbach, most of the trucks there were repaired, bringing the unit to almost complete functionality.

The 9th Ordnance Company failed the NWTI (Nuclear Weapons Technical Inspection) around that time and their responsibilities were transferred to the 64th. The 64th was in the process of retrograding the aging Nike-Hercules missiles to make way for the Pershing II system, but now had to take on the 9th's mission in addition to their own. They would fly air missions out of Fischbach to Ramstein Air Base to deliver the decommissioned Nike-Hercules warheads, pick up Pershing II warheads from the 9th in Miesau to take back to Fischbach, and fly the warheads back out of Fischbach to support units.

There was only one incident to report involving a crash of a CH-47 during the air missions, and it happened in Mannheim. All air missions were grounded until the cause of the crash was determined. When "walnut shell fragments" were discovered to be the cause of the crash, air missions resumed.

The 165th Military Police Company

The 165th Military Police Company was created in 1944 as a prisoner of war processing company. Official activation of the unit took place on October 25, 1944, at Fort Sam Houston in Texas. In 1945, it was redesignated as the 165th Military Police Escort Guard Company but was later deactivated the same year.

The 165th was reactivated on October 28, 1951, and stationed in Korea only to deactivate again in 1954. In 1962, the 165th was activated again, assigned first to the 193rd Ordnance Battaliothen placed under direct command of AWSCOM. In 1970, the 165th arrived at the Fischbach Army Depot.

The 165th MP Company is tasked with depot security. Approximately 80 soldiers were assigned to the 165th MP Company.

The 41st Ordnance Company (Detached)

The 41st Ordnance Company was activated in 1936 and assigned to the 1st Battalion, 32nd Quartermaster Regiment. It was redesignated as the 70th Quartermaster Battalion in 1940 and moved to Camp Gordon, Georgia, in 1942. The company was reorganized as the 3419th Ordnance Medium Automotive Maintenance Company in Europe and participated in four campaigns during World War II. The company deactivated in 1942.

The company was reactivated in in 1950 and participated in one campaign during the Korean War. In 1951, the unit was again deactivated.

The 41st Ordnance Company was activated in 1975 and stationed at Vogelweh as a part of the 72nd Ordnance Battalion.

In Fischbach, the 41st Ordnance Company Detachment was a missile maintenance company. Just as the 55Gs in Fischbach are tasked with nuclear warhead maintenance and support, missile techs from the 41st were tasked with missile maintenance and support, as warheads

3. Wilkommen in Deutschland

and missile propulsion units were stored separately. The 41st was responsible for the first and second stage propulsion units, which were stored in Area Two. The 41st did not work at Area One; they had their own separate site on the depot.

Our bus parked inside the front gate and I exited. A soldier standing there introduced himself as Wolton and asked if I was Woodward. I nodded the affirmative, and he instructed me to follow him.

We walked a few hundred feet to the barracks, where I was lead to a room on the second floor. The room was very well-kept, and the floor was buffed to a mirror finish. There was a full-size refrigerator in one corner, which surprised me. In the center of the room, a Persian style rectangular area rug was underneath a medium-size dining table complete with three chairs. A poster of Digital Underground was hanging over one of the bunks and one for the thrash band Slayer was hanging over the other. The third bunk was pushed against one of the windows; I assumed it was mine since there were no defining features. Wolton told me that my two roommates were also in M&A platoon and that the company likes to bunk us together. I would be sharing my room with Private First Class Merkins and Specialist Hooker, who were at the site and would be back to show me around the depot soon. In the meantime, I was to unpack my belongings and stow my gear in the wall locker.

"Do you live in the barracks too?" I asked Wolton.

"Nah, I live off base with my wife. We rent a small house in Fischbach. Get settled and we will have you over for dinner soon. In the meantime, chill here, and the guys will take care of you when they get back."

We shook hands, and Wolton left the room, closing the door behind him. I sat on my bunk, bouncing up and down to test the firmness. This room was more like a college dorm room than a military living quarters.

Merkins and Hooker arrived at the room at exactly 5 p.m. I jumped up from the bed as I heard the door handle open. They entered the room and greeted me with smiles. This small gesture quickly released the pent-up anxiety I had been storing. I shook their hands and gave them a quick once-over.

Merkins was an African American from Georgia. He was tall and his BDUs were a little baggy on his thin frame. His glasses were thick and the black frames even thicker. I could tell that he is good spirited and he offered to take me to the mess hall for chow after we talked a bit.

Appearance-wise, Hooker was the complete opposite of Merkins. He was a white guy, short, about five feet, eight inches, but heavily muscled. I could tell by looking at him that he spent most of his time at the gym. He was from the East Coast, but he didn't have as Eastern accent. When I told him I was from Chicago, he became excited and told me he was stationed at Fort Sheridan before he came to Fischbach. He also told me he had to get to the gym and we'd catch up later.

Merkins said it was time to eat, and I followed him from the room and down the stairs. Soldiers passed us either going up or coming down, and Merkins greeted each and every one of them. I could tell that he is well liked around the depot.

At the mess hall, I followed Merkins through the chow line. I was surprised to find out that meals were voluntary and we could eat wherever we choose. Some went to the EM club, others went off depot to local German restaurants, and some purchased food to keep in their refrigerators.

That evening at the mess hall, we had a choice of rabbit, a burger or macaroni and cheese. I had never heard of rabbit being a dish served for soldiers, let alone for those stationed at a small depot in southwestern Germany. In line, as I was deciding, the sergeant behind the Plexiglas spoke to me.

"New here?" he asks.

"Yes. I just can't decide what to have."

"Have some burgers tonight." He winked at me. I took his advice, and my food, back to the table.

Merkins began giving me the lowdown on the depot. As soldiers passed us, he told me their problems, if they're cool or not, and what jobs they have. I listened, just nodding my head. When his plate as empty, Merkins excused himself and went back to the counter. He spoke with the sergeant there and came back a few minutes later with another plate full of food. No rabbit, though. Just two more burgers. Merkins packed the food in, leaving me to wonder where it all went, he was so thin.

After the mess hall, we went back to the barracks. I stood outside to smoke a cigarette and was surprised to see two girls entering the

3. Wilkommen in Deutschland

back door. They did not look like soldiers, and they definitely were not American, judging by their style in clothes. They smiled at me as they passed and knocked on a door on the first floor. I watched as it opened, and they disappeared inside. I had just gotten my first close-up view of actual German females. I finished my cigarette and headed upstairs to my room. Merkins showed me where the latrine was, just down the hall. I got my shower gear together and walked to the latrine.

Music blasted from the rooms I passed. Metal from behind one door, rap from behind another. I entered the latrine and saw a row of stalls on the south wall and a corresponding row of sinks on the north wall. There was a brown paper bag filled with garbage under the utility sink on the wall, which I paused to stare at, wondering if the barracks were inspected each night, like they were in basic and AIT. Toward the back of the latrine were three shower stalls, relatively private. I showered then walked back to my room.

I spoke with Merkins until late at night, talking about music, food, girls, Chicago, Georgia or whatever else came to mind. We hit it off fairly well, and as midnight approached, I let sleep finally take me. I let a smile grow on my face, as I dreamt of the two German girls I saw today.

PT formation was at 6 a.m. sharp. I dressed in my Army-issue gray sweatshirt and sweatpants, and ran with Hooker and Merkins to formation, which was held in the parking lot in front of the HQ building. I fell in, took a spot in fourth squad, M&A platoon. Hooker was in fourth squad too, but Merkins was in second squad.

We started PT by doing the well-known "side straddle hop," or jumping jacks as they are called in the civilian world. This was followed by the turn and bounce, then squat thrusts. The Army had such colorful names for otherwise mundane exercises.

We finished with 20 push-ups, and then each platoon performed a right-face. The company colors were brought to the front of the formation. We then began the slow, familiar start of the morning run.

I always hated jogging, let alone running. I never grasped the concept of running aimlessly to stay in shape, when there were so many more interesting ways to develop cardiovascular strength.

We began at a slow jog, with the slowest runners at the front of the formation. This was my first time entering the depot proper, as we jogged past the guard at Area Two. Tall, branchless trees towered above us on both sides, and we began to sing cadences. I understood the philosophy of singing while running in formation; psychologically, it takes the soldier's mind from focusing on his sore feet, his lungs gasping for air, or his bursting heart. I enjoyed singing about "jumping out of C130s" (though I never did) and "eating mess hall cakes" (which I did). The songs lifted my spirits, and the voices singing in unison gave me strength.

Three miles into the run, I saw people begin to fall out of formation. We left them behind, took a turn onto another, smaller road, and began our return. Though it was January, it was about 40 degrees, and steam was coming from people's heads. I would have laughed if my heart wasn't beating so fast.

We returned to the barracks after PT, showered, and went to the mess hall for breakfast. It was only 7:30, and Hooker told me we didn't leave for the site until 8:30.

I ate quickly and went outside to smoke. Merkins arrived shortly after and told me I was needed at the HQ building. I followed him there and was introduced to one of the clerks who worked there, named

Area One secure site, 1993 (courtesy Wiebke Trott).

3. Wilkommen in Deutschland

Cretch. Cretch had me fill out some paperwork for my mailbox and also made me a laminated "blue border pass" to enter Area Two and a "black border pass" to enter Area One. It was almost 10 a.m. before we were finished, and I was worried about being late. Merkins laughed and told me not to worry. He had the keys to one of the VW vans assigned to the platoon. I jumped in the van with him, and he drove, first past the gate guard to Area Two, a German national in an olive green uniform carrying a pistol, who waved us through without looking at our IDs.

We drove deeper into the depot, and I marveled at the expanse of the expanse of it. Coming into a clearing, I saw a watchtower looming above, at tree height. The clearing opened up to a massive, fenced-in area.

This was it. The site. Area One.

4

Working Area One

Since the tank stoppers were already pulled from the concrete, Merkins drove the bus to the main gate. An MP stopped us and told us to go to the revolving gate. I passed though first, pushing on one of the thick bars to make the gate turn. Merkins followed, cracking jokes with the MP who stopped us. After I passed through the gate, I stood in front of a small, bulletproof window. Below the window was a stainless steel tray, not unlike the kind that gas stations in the city use to pass money or goods back and forth. I slid my black border pass into the tray and emptied my pockets, putting the contents into a small bucket. The MP inside of the guard shack looked at my pass, then slid it back into the tray.

"New here?" he asked.

"Yes, just got here."

"Well, welcome to Fort Fischbach," he said sarcastically, giving me back my belongings. Merkins followed suit, and I could see that he was very familiar with the guards. He laughed a few times, and I followed him to the end of the fenced-in walkway. A buzzer sounded and the gate opened. I followed Merkins to the bus and we drove toward the M&A building. He parked in front of the building and I followed him inside.

The first room just inside the front door was a break room. Typical military-style faux-leather chairs and a couch were present. I saw Hooker sitting on one of the chairs, reading a muscle magazine. On the other chair was a female; she stood up and gave me her hand.

"Sergeant Young. Nice to meet you," she said, smiling.

"Hello, Sergeant Young. Nice to meet you too." The anxiety began to wear off, and I relaxed.

"Everyone come up!" yelled Young through a doorway. Minutes later, the break room was filled with people.

4. Working Area One

"This is Woodward, he's new here. Introduce yourselves." I listened to the names, shaking hand after hand. The M&A platoon consisted of 20 soldiers, all nuke techs. It was a whirlwind of names and I try to remember as many as possible. What I noticed, while in the confines of the M&A building, was that the soldiers called each other by their first names. Last names were prominently displayed on tags on our BDUs, but everyone introduced themselves by their first names.

As I met everyone, two warrant officers entered the room from the bay area. One was tall and rather husky for a soldier. He had a cigarette hanging from the left side of his mouth and he took a seat on one of the chairs. He nodded at me, not saying a word. The other warrant officer came up and shook my hand.

"Chief Boyd, how are ya?"

I'm a bit taken aback with the informality. "Just fine, sir. Thank you."

"Just call me chief, it's okay," he replied, grinning.

"Ok chief," I responded.

He continued: "Someone go get Sergeant Kilgens. He's still in the back. And make some coffee." One of the techs ran in the bay and came back a few moments later with the oldest soldier I had ever seen.

Staff Sergeant Kilgens was the platoon sergeant, over 40 years old. He was wearing a battle patch on one sleeve, 25th Infantry Division. He also had a combat infantryman badge sewed onto his BDU shirt.

"How you doing, son?" he says to me. "Chief, can we start?" Kilgens pulled out a cigarette and lit it, slowly taking a drag. Chief Boyd nodded at Kilgens to begin.

Kilgens exhaled his cigarette smoke and began. "This here is Private Woodward. He will be assigned to fourth squad, projectile maintenance. Also, since Johnson ETSd, he will be the platoon M60 gunner."

I became excited; the others laughed. I did not notice it until then, but I was the lowest-ranked soldier in the platoon. Everyone was Private First Class (E-3) or above. Sergeant Kilgens was the ranking NCO. Even Staff Sergeant Washington, whom I arrived with, was also a staff sergeant. Chief Boyd was a CW1, and the other chief, who nodded at me when I first arrived, was a CW2, making him platoon leader.

Kilgens continued: "The missile crew will be going TDY [temporary duty] to Wertheim at the beginning of next month. The projectile crew will stay here and continue marking storage containers. Also,

Sergeant Badal will calibrate the radiac meters, and we will continue to train on the M422 and 155mm projectile as required.

"Next month's staff duty assignments are listed in the admin building. Woodward will start in a few weeks and will need someone to show him the ropes. Also, you all that house in the barracks will need to keep your rooms clean; there will be a battalion inspection in May. Other than that, take Woodward around, and help him settle in. That's it."

Kilgens managed to smoke three cigarettes in the two minutes it took him to brief the platoon.

The room cleared, and I was left with Merkins and Chief Boyd. Boyd wanted to take me on a perimeter tour, so he got on the phone to the main guard tower.

"This is Chief Boyd. We are leaving the building to inspect bunker doors. It will be me and Private Woodward." Muffled voice from other side of phone. "Yes, will do," replied Chief Boyd.

"Let's go," he said, motioning to me. I followed him outside and got in the passenger side of a camouflage-painted Chevy Blazer. He drove the road in front of the bunkers and began his tour speech.

"These bunkers contain the nukes that we maintain for the 7th Corps. You should be familiar with the weapons systems from your training at AIT. The M422, which we call the Old Eight-Inch, the M454, which we call the 1-5-5, and the Lance and Pershing II missile warheads." Chief Boyd slowed down and stopped in front of one of the bunkers. The grass covering the sides and top was brown and dead. A steel caged-in area, with two massive swing-out doors, secured access to the solid steel doors of the bunker itself.

"On site, we use the two-man rule. Always. That means, wherever you go, whether into the bays in the back of the M&A building, or outside of the building and in the site itself, you must be accompanied by another soldier. The large guard tower at the entrance keeps watch at the gate, and is the contact point for the MPs manning the towers around the perimeter. So far so good?"

"Sure thing, chief."

"All right." He began to drive again. "I am sure you're guessing what those poles are for." He swept his arm, and at that moment I noticed that all the grassy areas within the site were covered with eight-foot poles sticking in the ground. "Those are there to prevent unauthorized helicopter landings. There is one landing pad here on the site, used for

4. Working Area One

transporting nukes by air. And not too far away, on Thunder Road, a Hawk missile battery is located, which provides air defense against enemy aircraft or missiles."

My mind was swirling from all the information the chief was throwing at me. More was yet to come.

"Up there," he pointed at a large hill to the south with a rock formation at the top, which was relatively clear of trees. The formation looked like a solid rock wall with a ten-foot hole cut into it.

"That's called the 'Eye of Ludwigswinkel.' Germans go up there and look down into the site, trying to catch a glimpse of what's going on here. Most of them believe there are chemical and nerve agents stored here." The chief grinned. "If they only knew what was *really* here, they would probably have a bigger fit than what they are having at the moment."

"Are there chemical weapons here, chief?" I asked, as he pulled back into the parking space behind the building. He turned off the Blazer and looked at me.

Rear of M&A building with the Eye of Ludwigswinkel peering over Area One, 1993 (courtesy Wiebke Trott).

"No, just nukes. The chemical weapons are at Clausen, over near Münchweiler. You know how the military and politicians work. They neither confirm nor deny what is here. That keeps the locals guessing."

"As far as saying what is stored here, it is not forbidden to say anything. Hell, some of the soldiers here in the other platoons do not know exactly what is here, because they cannot access the site. Like I said, it is not a written rule to keep what is here secret. It's more like a bad kid or embarrassing uncle; we know their family, we just don't admit it. Got it?"

"Yes, chief." This seemed easy enough, and more exciting than I thought. I followed the chief's lead as he got out of the Blazer.

"Tomorrow we will be bringing in a couple of live Eight Incher's for maintenance. What we do is periodic inspection of the LLC [limited life components], test them or replace the components if needed. That is the crew you will be on, so you are going to be learning fairly quickly." I walked in the M&A building with the chief. He took me to the bay areas. He walked through the center bay and turned left to enter the first bay. Merkins was this bay with three others; there as a training container with a Pershing II partially lifted from it with a floor hoist (a "cherry picker"). They continued working on it without looking at us.

"First bay is the missile bay. First and second squads work here. They perform the maintenance on the Lances and Pershing IIs. Right now, they are repairing the ablative coating on one of them. Follow me." We walked through the center bay to the third bay. Hooker was there along with Sergeant Kilgens and another soldier named Thompkins. They were standing around a table with an M422 eight-inch shell on it. Hooker had his right hand inside the breechblock fuse area. He smiled at me when we entered.

"This is third bay, where the third and fourth squads work. This is the 'projectile' bay. See that enclosed area in the back?" I turned my head and saw a small 20-foot square area with waist-high wooden walls and Plexiglas topping them to a height of about eight feet.

"That is where the LLCs are handled. Proper protection will be required at all times while in there. It's no joke; follow the rules, please. It's better to be safe than to die by dry-land drowning from inhaling tritium. Got it?"

"Yes, chief," I responded.

"Good. Follow me." We left the bay area and passed through the break room to a room separated from the bays. There was electronic equipment everywhere: radiacs, oscillators, battery testers and a yellow chemical cabinet.

Sergeant Badal was in the room, smoking a cigarette while taking an ANPDR/60 apart. He nodded at me when we entered.

"This is the testing room. Sergeant Badal calibrates and tests our equipment, also repairs them when needed. In the corner, the yellow cabinet contains the chemicals and cleaning solutions we need to perform our duties. MolyBdenum, toluene, Freon, etc. Same stuff you used in AIT. Get it from Sergeant Badal as needed. Got it?"

It was overwhelming, but I got it.

"Got it, chief," I replied.

"Good. I have to get to staff duty, so go to your crew in the bay. See ya later, Woodward." I shook the chief's hand, and he left the building. I walked to the back, absorbing what I had been told and trying to grasp what is to come.

In the evening, I asked Hooker and Merkins if they wanted to go to the EM club. They didn't drink, so they declined. I walked down the stairs and out of the barracks. I followed the concrete stairs down the entrance of the club.

When I entered, music was playing loudly from the jukebox. You would think it was a Saturday night; the club was packed with soldiers, and every chair and booth was taken. I spotted an empty stool at the bar and took a seat. The bartender walked over to me. She was older, had short black hair, and asked me what I wanted to drink. I asked for a beer, and she returned with a Parkbrau Export in a half-liter bottle. I pulled out a cigarette, lit it, and turned to scan the room.

The club was a mix of male and female soldiers, boyfriends, girlfriends and German nationals. I could tell the Germans right away by their style of clothing, which differed from the traditional blue jeans and flannel shirts of the Americans.

I didn't know anyone yet, and I didn't want to come off as a flake by approaching total strangers.

"New here?" asked the guy sitting next to me. He was stocky with blonde hair, combed to a part on the side, and wearing glasses.

"Yes," I responded, taking a drag from the cigarette.

"I'm Kaminski," he said, and I shook his hand. "What platoon are you in?"

"M&A." My beer was almost empty, and I could feel a buzz. The bartender asked me if I wanted another, and I nodded at her.

"Ah, a 'glow worm.' Cool. I'm a 55B. Ammo specialist. You liking it here so far?" I could tell Kaminski was half drunk, as his speech was slurred.

"Yeah, so far so good." I took a long swallow of the beer. I had never experienced real German beer before, and the taste was electrifying.

As if reading my mind, Kaminski continued. "The beer is awesome and the girls are even better. On Thursday nights we go to a club in Niederschlettenbach, a town not too far from here. We just call it 'Nieder' for short. And on the weekends, we go to the rolling disco. I have a car, so you can drive with us this Saturday night. I'll introduce you around."

I thanked him and sat there talking the night away. It was almost midnight before I returned to the barracks, stumbling up the stairs and down the hallway until I found my room, where I plopped into bed, fully clothed.

We left for the site early the next day. Arriving at the gate, I was told to pull the tank stoppers out. I struggled at first, while the others got a laugh from me struggling with them. The rest of the crew walked to the turnstile, and we showed our passes and emptied our pockets. I was called as the "number of the day," and I got pulled inside the guard building, once again to the amusement of the others.

The MPs were geared up because we were moving nukes that day. The one searching me ran his hands up and down my arms and legs, patting me down. I got released a few minutes later and jumped into the VW bus.

The break room was filled with MPs and nuke techs. I didn't know what really was happening, so I clung to Hooker for guidance. He was given two long chains by an MP, from each of which a thin, red aluminum bar dangled. On the bars were random holes drilled completely through and stamped-on numbers. Hooker puts the chains over his head and wears them like a necklace.

"These are the bunker keys," he said to me.

The same MP also gave me two sets of keys, mine yellow. I followed Hooker's lead and put them over my head. Specialist Thompkins and Sergeant Kilgens were also issued keys.

"Ready, everyone?" asked one of the MPs. They were decked out in complete battle gear, and completely serious in their duty.

4. Working Area One

Chief Boyd responded the affirmative.

The MPs opened the building door, and Hooker picked up a small hand jack and handle from the floor, motioning me to follow the MPs and himself, while Thompkins and Sergeant Kilgens followed close behind with their escorts. The MPs led us toward a bunker, and Sergeant Kilgens and Thompkins split off and followed their escorts to a different bunker.

We stopped in front of our bunker, and the MP radioed the tower.

"Go time?"

Static then a muffled voice over the radio. "Go time in two minutes. Hold steady."

The MP addressed us. "We have to wait two more minutes."

"What's going on?" I asked, thoroughly confused.

"The Soviets have a satellite passing overhead. In two minutes it will be clear. We will then be able to access the bunker, and retrieve the device." I giggled when he said device.

"If you get the device in time, we can go straight to the M&A building. If not, we will have to wait again for another satellite to pass overhead."

"Got it," I replied.

Hooker and I just stood there, not saying a word. The two minutes seemed like an eternity. I was just about to crack a joke about Hooker's mother when the radio crackled.

"Clear. We have a window."

"10-4," replied the MP escort. "Let's go."

We followed the escort to the bunker's security cage. The MP pulled out a key and unlocked the cage door. We helped him swing it out and stepped inside the caged area. In front of us were two massive, solid steel bunker doors. Hooker motioned me to a black box on the bunker wall, near the right door. He fumbled at the key hanging around his neck, and then stuck it into a slot in the top of the black box. Air hissed from somewhere, startling me.

"Now you," Hooker said. I stuck my key into the second slot, and more air hissed, then a loud *clunk-clunk-clunk*. The air stopped, and Hooker bent down and put the hand jack underneath the door hinge. He began pumping the jack with the handle, and I noticed the door rising an inch at a time. When bottom of the door cleared the concrete pad, Hooker swung the door open.

Steel bunker entrance with WADS system, 1993 (courtesy Wiebke Trott).

4. Working Area One

"Let's go," he said. The MP stood outside of the door and did not enter the bunker.

The bunker was dimly lit inside. There was concertina wire hanging from the ceiling which creeped me out. Hooker noticed me staring at it.

"This is part of the WADS [Weapons Access Delay System]. If the bunker gets breached, the guards in the main building can activate the alarm, which causes the razor wire to fall on whoever is inside. Then smoke is released, while the terrorists or Soviets or whoever is trapped underneath, incapacitated." Hooker swiped his finger across his neck. "It's a guaranteed death sentence. Plain and simple. Let's get moving."

The WADS project was created in 1984, with the U.S. Army spending $34 million to add the security system to bunkers across Europe that housed nuclear weapons. There were 5,800 American tactical nuclear weapons in Europe, with 3,800 of them Army nuclear projectiles and missiles and the rest Air Force bombs. In the 1980s, there was a growing concern on Capitol Hill and in the Pentagon that the nuclear warheads, some of which could be carried by a single man, were tempting targets for terrorists. The M454 and M422 were older model nukes and did not have electronic security devices that allowed them to be destroyed by remote control radio signal if stolen. The Pentagon developed the WADS system to protect the aging nuclear weapons.

The nuke containers were lined up in perfect rows, reminding me of a morning formation. There were 25 containers in all, each with a yellow outline of a rectangle around them.

"This is the 'one meter rule.' Anyone not actively involved in moving or working on the nuke needs to stay outside of the rectangle, to reduce radiation exposure."

I walked with him to the back of the bunker, and we took a flat, four-wheeled cart and pushed it toward the container we needed to move. We each took a side, lifted the container onto the cart, and pushed it toward the front of the bunker. We moved it outside, into the caged area. Hooker swung the door shut and released the jack, allowing the door to fall back into place. We then performed our key sequence and the air locks engaged, securing the door.

"We have to wait, you all," said the MP. "Got another five minutes to go." While we waited, I tried to think of the joke I was going to make about Hooker's mother. My mind was blank, and I strained to remember until the MPs voice called out.

WADS system inside bunker, 1993 (courtesy Wiebke Trott).

4. Working Area One

"All's clear. Let's move."

I strained with Hooker to push the cart, and I saw that Sergeant Kilgens and Specialist Thompkins were almost to the M&A building. It took about ten minutes for us to reach the back of the building, which also had a caged-in area. We pushed the cart into the enclosed area then through the garage door into the third bay.

The MPs were not allowed access to the bays when live nuclear weapons were present. Guards were posted at the entrance door to the bays inside the building. Their guard duty consisted of smoking cigarettes and gabbing with whoever was in the break room at the moment.

I wheeled the cart to the back of bay three, putting in next to the cart that Sergeant Kilgens and Thompkins wheeled in. We put on our white protective suits, and gloves, which we fastened tight to our forearms with duct tape, or, as it is known in the Army, "100 mile an hour tape."

All four of us began with one container. I helped Hooker lift the lid, and we set it off to the side. We then stood the projectile straight up in the container and secured it at the bottom so it did not tip over.

We then removed the nose cone, which housed the components we needed to inspect. Kilgens and Thompkins stood to the side and passed tools to us, quickly stepping back after they handed over the tools we needed.

When the job was complete, I placed the nose cone back onto the projectile and turned it clockwise until it was securely fastened. We laid the weapon back down in its container and secured the lid. Sergeant Kilgens ran the radiac meter over the outside of the container, watching the needle on the dial. He nodded to us when finished, and we pushed the container against the wall. We then reversed roles for the second container; this time Hooker and I were passing tools back and forth to Kilgens and Thomkins.

When they were complete, I ran the radiac meter over the container. I held the meter in my right hand, keeping it at about an inch about the container, sweeping it back and forth the length of the container. In my left hand I held the reader and watched the needle jump back forth, always below the hazard line. Alpha radiation readings were normal, and the needle just barely reached the beta radiation mark. I nodded at Sergeant Kilgens, and he pushed the cart next to the other container.

With the job finished, we reversed the steps we took earlier, always waiting for unseen Soviet satellites to pass overhead, and always under the watchful gaze of the military police in guard towers and as escorts.

Before the workday finished, we ere debriefed by Chief Boyd and Sergeant Kilgens. Everything went well, no nuclear disasters or accidental shootings happened, so we were successful. Next week, the missile crew would be performing maintenance on Pershing II warheads.

I still had an adrenaline rush when we get back to the barracks. It was Friday, and Hooker suggested we go sightseeing and head to Paris over the weekend. It was only a four-hour drive from Fischbach, and we could make it there and back by Tuesday.

"What about Monday formation?" I asked him. I had no desire to miss a formation and get called out of ranks.

"I'll drive to Kilgens' house tonight and ask him if we can have the day off. He'll say yes, don't worry. See ya." Like a whirlwind he was out of our room. While he was gone, I packed a few items and tried to fall asleep.

I dreamed of an explosion and characters running around in Mad Max–style clothing. The ground was burnt black, with embers casting a dull orange glow on the charred branches of decimated trees. Lightning crackled, outlining those characters who were running around shooting at each other. Some little kids were huddled together against an old Dumpster, crying as grasshoppers with mouths full of fangs began to crawl over them...

I jumped up and grabbed my chest. My dog tags chimed as they rattled against each other. I looked at the alarm clock, and the red digital numbers showed 4:30 a.m. I looked over at Hooker's bunk and saw he was still asleep.

"Hooker," I whispered. "Hooker, time to go, man." I looked over at Merkins' bunk and noticed it hadn't been slept in. His girlfriend lived on the first floor, and he must have stayed with her.

"Hooker," I said louder. "Let's go, man!" Hooker finally rolled over and opened his eyes.

"All right man, damn." He slowly got up, and I left the room to get ready.

By 5:15, we were on the road in Hooker's 1977 BMW 316. It was bright green, very well taken care of. We took the Autobahn, traveling the maximum speed his car could go: 90 mph. Newer Mercedes passed

4. Working Area One

us like we were standing still. In Germany, the left lane was used for passing only. You were not allowed to pass on the right, and the left lane traffic had to always be going faster than the right lane traffic. It made perfect sense to me, and I wished that America would make such a law.

Once we passed through Saarbruecken, we hit the French border and jumped on the A4 expressway, which would take us directly to Paris.

Verdun

Two and half hours into the trip, I saw a sign for the town of Verdun. I asked Hooker if he knew what happened there in World War I, and he had no clue. I told him to drive there; it was still early and I wanted to see it.

A small city, during the First World War Verdun was the epitome of suffering and death. The Battle of Verdun between the Germans and French in 1916 lasted for ten months and claimed more than 300,000 lives. It was the bloodiest battle of World War I in terms of wounded and dead, and it was psychologically devastating to those who survived.

We stood in front of a large monument, a set of statues depicting five French soldiers, each bearing different weapons and uniforms of the French military. We took photos standing in front of it and noticed a uniformed soldier also getting his photo taken in front of the monument.

Hooker, never shying away from meeting new people, walked up to the soldier and asked if he spoke English. He said he did, and in broken English we began a conversation. He was a French soldier on leave, and he wanted to come see the monument with his family. When he learned we were American soldiers, he became excited and started asking questions.

"Are you Special Forces? Do you know Captain Hallister? I met him in Paris. He was in Vietnam. Where are you from? What do you do in the Army?"

I became amused, and Hooker began answering his questions, telling the French soldier that he is a Green Beret and just back from Panama. The Frenchman looked at me, and I recalled what Chief Boyd told me in the Blazer as we drove around the site.

"I ... uh ... I clean toilets." A stare, then a loud laugh. Hooker joined him in the laughter. When it died down, the French soldier quickly blurted out: "I clean toilets too."

After politely refusing a lunch invitation several times with the French soldier and his family, we said goodbye and got back on the road to Paris.

Paris

It was dusk when we saw the Parisian lights, and we found a parking spot just south of the Eiffel Tower. We had no idea where we were going, so we started by wandering around, taking in the sights and people. The City of Light lived up to its name, and I was totally bewildered with the city. We stopped at an outdoor cafe and gobbled up bread with soft cheese and red wine, admiring the stylish girls, tourist and French alike, who passed by us. Hooker tried to call out to a few, but they simply laughed and kept walking. I snapped a couple of shots of the Eiffel Tower from a distance, and we continued walking north, crossing the Seine River, following George V Avenue. There was a place here that Hooker wanted to stop and see: the Crazy Horse, Paris, France, as celebrated by Vince Neil in the Mötley Crüe song "Girls, Girls, Girls." "That's where we're going first," he said. "I just gotta find it."

We continued walking, and to our luck, spotted some teenagers standing at a corner. Hooker asked them if anyone spoke English and where the Crazy Horse bar was. Luck was with him; one did speak English, and he walked us about a block north and then stopped and pointed. In bright red neon, the words "Crazy Horse" lit up the street above an entrance in a row of upscale shops.

Hooker pulled me eagerly toward the building, and standing at the entrance was a man dressed in a Canadian Mounties uniform. Hooker made me take a photo of him with one arm around the Mountie and the other arm flexing a muscle. It was all good fun until we tried to enter. The Mountie told us that we were underdressed; no jeans allowed. Hooker pleaded with him, giving him a sob story about traveling all the way from the United States to come to this establishment. A few minutes of begging, and the Mountie relented and let us in.

We passed through the vestibule where souvenirs were sold and

4. Working Area One

walked straight into the showroom. The room was dimly lit, and round tables covered in white linen were randomly placed in front of a stage. Candles glowed from each table, adding to the ambiance of the room.

I walked with Hooker to the bar and took a menu. It was written in English and French, and my eyes scanned over it, locking on words written in bold red letters: *$80 per drink, minimum two.*

I showed Hooker the menu, and he shrugged. The bartender, clad in a white button-up shirt and red bowtie, asked us what we were drinking. We were one Jack and Coke with two straws. I handed over the money, and we turned to look at the stage. The room got quiet as the red curtain went up.

I really had no idea what to expect at the Crazy Horse, and I definitely did not know it was a cabaret show, and a *high-class* cabaret show at that. A line of women wearing fishnet stockings, high heels and black tutus formed on the stage. They were also topless. They began their routine, and the audience erupted with applause. Men in Armani suits with bottles of expensive champagne clapped along with the music as the girls danced.

I bobbed my head to the music and took the glass of Jack Daniels from Hooker. I sipped on the straw, and nothing came up. I shook the glass, and there was only ice rattling around the bottom. It was empty.

"Let's get out of here," I said, not really wanting to leave, but knowing that we couldn't spend any more money in there. Hooker agreed, and we set the glass down on the bar and headed toward the vestibule. We saw the Mountie standing inside the door, and Hooker waved at him. He waved back, and we made our exit.

The Arc de Triomphe was not too far away, so we walked over to it to take photos. Once again, Hooker stood there, flexing as I took the photo. When it was my turn, I just stood there in my black and white cardigan, smiling. We then walked back in the direction of the car and stopped at the Eiffel Tower. The structure towered over us, and hundreds of people were still milling about, even though it was past midnight. We paid the $40 to ride the elevator to the first floor and took photos of the city from every direction. We then stood in line to ride the elevator to the top and noticed it would cost another $40 to get up there. We decided against it and headed back down.

In front of the Eiffel Tower was a long, grassy park. We found a park bench, and Hooker lay down on it, exhausted. I took the bench next to his. It seemed only moments that my eyes were closed, when someone woke us with a kick. I sat up quickly and saw two French policeman standing in front of us. They were yelling in French, and we had no idea what they were yelling about. Hooker told them in English that we were Americans. One policeman then switched to English.

"No sleeping here. Move on."

We got up slowly, apologizing and moving on.

"I'm too tired to drive, man," said Hooker. "Can you?"

"Nah. I'm beat." I realized we really hadn't thought this trip out. We had little money and nowhere to sleep. We started walking toward the car again, and Hooker took a turn into an alley. I followed him, and he stopped and pointed. There was a metal fire-escape ladder, and he began to climb it. I followed, and we ended up on a small landing on the backside of a building. We lay down and got into small talk, just then hearing voices underneath us in the dark. We peeked over the landing and saw what looked like homeless people just below us, stretching out in the alley. Hooker got the bright idea of tossing coins down at them. Within seconds, they were being pelted by coins. We jumped back every time they start to look up, silently laughing. We decided to stop before they discovered us and quickly fell asleep.

We woke a few hours later, and I decided to drive us home. As we passed Verdun, which for me was much more hauntingly interesting than Paris, I thought of all those dead soldiers, littering the countryside as cannon shells tore them to pieces. I tried to grasp the destruction that had taken place in this region in the last hundred years, and it was a concept, as an American, that was hard to understand.

Tuesday morning we fell into formation, and after the company reports, we began to tell the others of our experience in France. Sergeant Kilgens interrupted just as I was going over how to give change to homeless people the correct way. Next week, he barked, we were going to Baumholder to weapon qualify, including the M60. I was excited as the others mumbled under their breath. I had been itching to fire that monster ever since it was assigned to me.

We spent the week training on our projectiles, while first and second squads performed their annual maintenance on the missile warheads. We took a break every hour or so, and I sat down in the break room with Hooker, Sergeant Kilgens, Specialist Thompkins, Sergeant Badal, and Chief Boyd.

4. Working Area One

The sergeant I arrived at Fischbach with, Sergeant Washington, had already left; he had a serious family matter to attend to and was granted a new station back in the States.

Two MPs were standing guard at the door to the bays, looking bored and using their M16s to prop themselves up.

Suddenly there was yelling from inside the bays. First and second squads came running through the door, with Merkins herding them out. The MPs freaked out; one grabbed his weapon and pointed it at the door, while the other swung the heavy steel door shut and secured it. They were yelling, "What happened? What's going on?" One of them was about to get on the radio, when Merkins, out of breath, told him to wait. Those of us who were in the break room, including the MPs, were totally confused. I was starting to freak out.

Did they drop a warhead? Did someone go ballistic and sneak a weapon inside? Did massive amounts of radiation get released?

I began to scare myself. Everyone was looking at Merkins, and I saw a sly grin begin to creep up on his face.

Chief Boyd could no longer control himself. He yelled, "Merkins, what the hell is going on?"

"Nothing, Chief," responded Merkins nonchalantly. He regained his breath and said almost casually: "We saw a mouse."

The mouse incident was just one of many insane events that happened at the site. I was told that years ago, one of the watchtower guards from the 165th spotted something moving in the forest behind the bunkers. He radioed the sighting in, and an alert was sounded. When the guard commander asked the MP what he saw, he responded that it was large and white, but he couldn't make out exactly what is was. The military took nuke site security seriously, and the MPs were more than willing to follow up. They sent out an armed squad into the forest to find the white monster, which, according to legend, they never found.

Another event happened in either the late 1970s or early 1980s. An MP was sitting in his tower, when he claimed a disc-shaped UFO hovered above the site for 30 seconds, causing a power outage. It then sped off, and the power was restored, as if nothing had happened. There were several witnesses, but none of them were currently stationed in Fischbach. I took both of the accounts with a grain of salt.

UFOs I get, and I can see odd occurrences happening, though I would think the missile battery in Salzwoog would have picked up something on their radar.

Snow monsters? They were a completely different category of sightings. Life at Fischbach was boring, the depot separated from the rest of the world by fences and miles of road. I believe the MPs were sent annually for psychological testing, to see if the individual soldier was still mentally fit to perform his duty. Maybe the military should have augmented the testing with monster and UFO identification for MP units stationed near nuke sites.

One Saturday night I rode with Kaminski to the Rolling Disco, which was being held in Bundenthal. I was introduced to a German named Georg, who was a familiar face around the depot. I took an instant liking to him, and he practiced his English on me, while I practiced my German.

Kaminski introduced me to different German alcoholic drinks. The first one I tried was called a Filo, white wine and Sprite mixed together. I drank the glass quickly before being introduced to Filo's cousin, the Rocco, red wine and Coke mixed together, and chugged it too. My head swam instantly, and the others began to laugh and slap me on the back.

I was then handed a beer, which, when I tasted it, was very sweet. I nodded in approval, and Georg told me it was a Radler, Sprite and beer mixed together, supposed to help prevent hangovers by hydrating the body while drinking, or so they told me.

There were other Americans present, some from Fischbach who I had seen before around depot but had never spoken to. There were also Americans from Camp Dahn we didn't talk to.

Standing there drinking with Kaminski and Georg, I felt a shove to my back. I stumbled forward and turned around. An angry guy stood there, and he shoved me again.

"What the hell?" I shouted at him. "What the hell's your problem?" He shoved me again, and my beer spilled on the floor. Though drunk, I recognized him as soldier from Fischbach, one I had never spoken to before.

"Are you serious?" I yelled, as he shoved me again.

"Yeah, I'm serious!" He rushed forward, just as a fist came flying from the corner of my eye and hit my attacker in the face. He fell down, and Georg stood over him. He got up, holding his face, and walked back to his friends who were sitting at another bench.

4. Working Area One

"Dude, thanks," I said to Georg. I had no idea what that was all about. I didn't bump into the guy, I didn't say anything to him to make him upset, hell, I didn't even look at him. It came out of left field.

"I could have handled him," I said, trying to save face. "Why did you jump in?"

Georg looked at me as if I was joking, and said, "He spilled your beer."

I spent most of Sunday in bed with a massive hangover. It was almost 5 p.m. before I crawled out of bed, my throat dry but my stomach still not hungry. So much for Filo being the anti-hangover drink.

Monday morning we rode the bus to Baumholder dressed in full battle gear. Baumholder was home to the 8th Infantry Division (Mechanized), which had been stationed in Baumholder and the surrounding communities since the 1950s. It was a vast kaserne, surrounded by rolling hills and forests, and it also included a military airstrip.

We headed to the range and began to set up our equipment. The M60 was heavy, weighing just over 23 pounds unloaded. Specialist Thompkins was my assistant gunner and carried the ammunition, spare barrel and bipod.

We set up on an embankment, looking over a grassy area with a small pond. On a cliff on the other side, about 700 yards out, were full body targets silhouettes.

The four platoons of the 64th set up our weapons. I took a prone position and opened the feed tray. Thompkins unraveled the ammunition belt and laid the end onto the tray, which I closed. We were told to lock and load, and I pulled back on the feed lever to chamber the first round.

I squeezed the trigger, holding it down for three seconds, then releasing. The gun butted against me hard, but I liked the heaviness of it. It was solid, and the bipod made it much easier to control than if it was free standing.

"Wide to the right," said Thompkins. I adjusted my sighting and fired again. The burst of rounds hit the target, and it fell over. I moved my sights to the next target. *Rat-at-at-at-at-at...* the target went down. As did the third and fourth. We needed to hit all five targets to qualify, and as I was sighting the target to finish the qualification, small, black objects began to fly upwards from the pond. As if on cue, machine gun fire burst out as the other soldiers began taking shots at the black objects, which turned out to be ducks. The air was crackling around me as they kept firing, trying to hit something besides air.

"Cease fire! Cease fire!" commanded the range master. The crackling stopped; it became deathly quiet.

The range master jumped down from his small tower and called a formation. We jumped up and left our weapons lying on the ground.

He was a burly man, and, judging by his character, one of the infantryman stationed here. He began yelling, I mean literally screaming at the top of his lungs about professionalism and integrity, and commanded everyone to drop to the front leaning rest position. None of us moved at first; maybe the combat arms NCOs treated their soldiers like raw recruits, but we were the 64th, inhabitants at Fort Fischbach, and, on top of that, Thompkins and I were nuke techs.

None of those things mattered to a grunt. He yelled even louder, and we dropped down. He began counting cadence, and we pushed up and down and up and down. It seemed never-ending, and I felt my arms tiring.

"On your feet!" he commanded, just as my arms gave out. He walked over to Sergeant Kilgens, who had been watching from the side of our bus. The two shook hands, and the infantry NCO looked at us, shook his head, then walked away.

Back on the bus, Sergeant Kilgens addressed everyone present. He told us that combat arms soldiers were trained differently than ordnance, and that they had their own set of rules and etiquette. Kilgens would know: he was in the 25th Infantry Division in Vietnam. He finished up by telling us we all qualified and then he added with a smile, "Four M60 gunners, and not one of you hit a damn duck."

5

Familiar Faces

In July 1990, my mother and grandparents flew to Germany to visit me. I asked for a few days of leave and drove with them in their rented Mercedes to a small *Gasthaus* in Dahn-Reichenbach, about 20 kilometers from the depot. My German friend Georg lived there. His aunt owned the *Gasthaus* and let my family stay there for $15 a night, including breakfast.

I dropped them off for the evening and came back early the next morning. They were eating breakfast, soft-boiled eggs, rolls and assorted cheeses and lunchmeat, with my friend's aunt at the small dining table. The aunt was old, a child during World War II. My grandfather was in the Army Air Force during the war and sent to Germany. I struggled to translate for them when she said she feared the Americans but didn't hate them. I told her we were all friends now and this was a different time. She nodded, and I wondered if she was just being polite or nodding in an affirmation that we were not there to cause harm.

After breakfast, I took my family to a war museum in the building next to the gasthaus, also owned by Georg's family. I showed them the different weapons and uniforms of the German army and finished the tour by sitting on an anti-aircraft gun that had a concrete plug in the barrel but could still pivot and turn 360 degrees.

We went across the street to a small pub run by an older German named Fritz. I had been in the pub many times with Georg. The owner was very friendly and sat with us as my family sampled Parkbräu, the local beer.

Like Georg's aunt had earlier, Fritz began to speak about the war. He was 16 when he was drafted into the army in 1944 and became an officer. The Germans were low on manpower by that time, and Fritz was sent to the Eastern Front. He was captured by the Russians and treated brutally. He liked to repeat his survivor story when he was tipsy. The Russians had a huge pit dug into the ground where they kept POWs. As the captured Germans walked to the ladder that led to the bottom of the pit, a Russian held the barrel of his rifle and swung the butt as hard as possible, hitting each German in the head as he crouched to grab the ladder. Fritz was about eighth in line and started panicking because his turn was coming up. With minutes left to decide a plan of action, Fritz turned around and punched the German soldier behind him in the face. Naturally, the soldier retaliated, and a fight broke out. The Russians then grabbed both Fritz and the other German soldier he fought with and *pushed* them both into the pit, sparing a whack to the head with a rifle butt and possible death.

The next day, I drove my family to the city of Basel, Switzerland, which was only a two-hour drive from the Fischbach. Basel was a beautiful medieval city situated on the Rhine River at the border of Germany and France. We spent the day shopping and snapping photos before heading back to Germany.

To get the full three-country tour, the next day I took them to Wissembourg, France.

Wissembourg

Later that evening, we had dinner at a Croatian restaurant in Dahn. The proprietor was ecstatic to find out my grandparents were both American *and* Croatian. They spoke Croatian with the owner of the restaurant, and the food suddenly appeared in a heaping pile on the table, along with a bottle of red wine. The restaurant was empty that night, so the owner sat with us. The table spoke Croatian for the most part, then switched to German or broken English when anyone wanted to speak with me or my mother.

Shots of slivovica (Croatian plum brandy) were brought to the table after dinner, and we toasted each other, *Zivio!* After the shots, the table got silent for a moment. The owner started to speak about an upcoming war in Croatia against the communist Serbs. If I wanted, he could get me a passport to go down there and fight when it starts.

I was taken aback as the restaurant owner looked at me. The silence was deafening. This was not my fight. We may have had relatives in Gospič and Glina, but I had no desire to go to Croatia to fight in a war I didn't understand.

I politely declined the offer, telling him I am in the United States Army, and that is where my obligations are. I was relieved when the owner nodded and began to laugh. We took another shot of slivovica and called it a night.

My mother and grandparents stayed a week, then left for Frankfurt, where they were going to visit Croatian relatives. I kissed them goodbye and watched the Mercedes speed away, sad but also happy to see them leave.

Staff duty in Fischbach was performed in the admin building, located in Area Two. Outside of the staff officer, the PFC, specialist or sergeant performing staff duty is the ranking soldier on the depot (during night hours for the most part).

The duty office was a small room across from the armory. It contained a desk, with a STU-III (secure telephone unit), a couch and a television set, which was perched in the corner on a small shelf. In the back of the office was another room, where a communications specialist sat in front of a TacSat (tactical satellite). The TACSAT received a "pulse" every 15 minutes, to which the commo specialist had to respond. This was SOP (standard operating procedure) at every nuke depot in the world. In the event of no response, a phone call would come through, which the staff duty personnel would have to answer. If there was still no answer, a response team of MPs were sent to the site to investigate.

Also in the commo room were two safes; one contained EAMs (emergency action messages), and the other contained a decoding book. There were two locks on each safe, with the staff duty NCO knowing one combination, and the staff duty officer knowing the other.

It was a hot summer morning at the end of July 1990, and I was assigned to staff duty. The shift began at 7:00 and ran for 24 hours until 7:00 the next morning. I was paired with a second lieutenant, who only arrived at Fischbach a month before. His name was Lieutenant Westmayer, and he was a 55B (ammunition specialist). He was also the platoon leader for Alpha platoon. He lifted weights constantly, keeping himself in shape. Where Hooker was huge muscle-wise, Westmayer was massive. I didn't say anything off color to him, though I had to stop myself from calling him Lt. Butterbar to his face. "Butterbar" is slang for a second lieutenant, because the officer rank bar is gold. They were essentially the "privates" of commissioned officers, either fresh out of college or straight out of OCS (Officer Candidate School).

I showed up for duty after breakfast and saw that my commo buddy for the shift was this pretty blonde who lived on the first floor of the barracks. She was a specialist, and I had only talked to her once or twice in the past. She greeted me with a smile, and we began chatting about life, Fischbach, the Army, Germans, and so on.

The admin building was hustle and bustle that day. I looked out of the Plexiglas window, which peered into the admin bay. The armorer was in his cage, passing out rifles to soldiers who were either going to duty or leaving for TDY. I called out to him, though I couldn't see him in his cage.

"Yo, Iverson, throw me my gun and my knife!" The Army hated it when you called your rifle your "gun" and your bayonet your "knife." This had been drilled into us since basic training. Armorers hated it even more.

"Shut the hell up, Woodward!" he yelled back. I saw Iverson regularly at the NCO club, and we drank together often. He was a fun guy to be around, and we got along great.

The day drug on as I sat there with nothing to do. I listened to Specialist Baar type on the TACSAT keypad every 15 minutes, which made the day go by even slower, as I counted the times she hit the keys.

The hours passed and the traffic died down in the admin building. Lt. Westmayer returned. He came in the office and asked if anything had came up, emergencies or the like. I told him negative, and he retired to the staff officer room, which was just down the hall. That room was even more depressing than the one we were in; it was a large storage room with a cot against the wall. Staff officers were allowed to sleep during the night, while we needed to stay awake.

Five o'clock came, and I needed to make a troop strength report to battalion. We used the STU-III for secure connections.

The STU-III was developed by the NSA as a secure means of voice communication of non-secure analog telephone networks. To initiate a secure call, the parties on both ends of the line secured it by inserting a CIK (crypto ignition key) into a slot on the phone. When the keys were turned by both parties, the line was secure.

5. Familiar Faces

I dialed the number for battalion. A male voice answered on the other end.

"This is Private First Class Woodward, 64th Ordnance Company, ready to report."

"Proceeding with the secure connection. Initializing in 3-2-1...."

I turned the CIK, and there was a brief pause as white noise developed over the line.

"Report, Private."

"280 assigned, ten on leave, five on TDY and five on sick call. That is all." I waited for the confirmation.

"Report received. Ending secure connection." The phone crackled, and I turned the key.

"Good evening, private."

"Goodbye," I responded, never knowing the face on the other side of the line.

After the call, I put a Steven Seagal tape into the VCR. Baar sat with me as we watched *Above the Law*. I had never seen aikido before, and it was truly amazing to watch Segal move so smoothly. Just as he was about to stop some CIA agents from cutting off a Viet Cong's foot, the phone rang.

"Staff Duty," I answered, annoyed at being interrupted.

"I need staff officer now! This is Sergeant Black!" I knew Sergeant Black and did not care for him much. He was an MP with the 165th and a hardcore soldier. He barked instead of spoke, and he had tried to boss me around a couple of times.

"This is Private Woodward. How can I help you, sergeant?" I say smugly.

"Get me the staff officer now!" he screamed. My face flushed red.

"Don't let your rank get confused with my authority, sergeant. What do you need?" I said rather haughtily.

"Dammit, I need the duty driver—I have a soldier throwing up blood!"

"Relax, sergeant, I'm getting him on the line now." I picked up the walkie-talkie we used to get in touch with the staff duty driver, who stayed in a room in the barracks.

"Smythe, you there?" I released the button on the side of the walkie-talkie. Seconds later, Smythe responded.

"Yeah, Woody. I'm here."

"Go down to the MP barracks. Sergeant Black will meet you there with one of his guys that has to go to the hospital. Take him to Münchweiler. Call me when you get there."

"All right, man, be right down."

I went back to the phone. "Sergeant Black, the driver will meet you in front of the barracks."

"Woodward...," I could sense fuming on the other side of the phone, "this isn't over."

"Goodnight, sergeant," I replied and hung up the phone. I knew it was an empty threat, since Black is PCSing (permanent change of station) in a couple of weeks and won't risk getting an Article 15 by knocking me out.

The vomiting soldier situation taken care of, I resumed the movie with Baar. We stopped the movie several times to talk, and I found out her family was Dutch and she could speak the language. We talked well into the night, until the crypto machine next to the STU-III began to buzz. I jumped up and rushed to it. It was a small white crypto-tape machine, with lights that blink red and green. I stood there, and a tape came out of the machine. I ran out of the office and banged on the staff officer's door.

"Sir, get up, please. We have a message." I heard Westmayer fumbling about in the dark, and he came out in his brown t-shirt and BDU pants. We rushed back to the office and into the back room.

I stood at the cabinet safe, turned away from it with my hand on the safe door to make sure it did not open without both of us watching. I heard Westmayer turning the dial on the combination lock, and with a click, it opened. I then turned around and bent down to enter my combination. Westmayer turned his body and placed his hand on the door. The combination lock clicked open, and I set it off to the side. We then opened the safe drawer and matched the numbers on the crypto tape to one of the EAM packets. We took it out and Westmayer tore it open. It had random letters and numbers in horizontal rows the length of the card.

To decipher the message, we need the codebook, which was in another safe on the floor. We repeated the steps we took with the cabinet safe, and Westmayer took out a book with a white cover and orange letters: "Top Secret."

I sifted through the pages and found the correct page corresponding

5. Familiar Faces

to the EAM code. We began the deciphering process, matching letters and numbers in the book with those on the EAM. It was like using a decoder ring from a cereal box. The letters started to make words and I was excited beyond belief. This could be it. Something had happened in the world or was about to happen, and I was one of the select people, outside of the president and CIA, who was privy to the details. I scanned quickly, writing the words down...

"TEST. THIS IS ONLY A TEST. NOTHING ELSE FOLLOWS."

"Dammit!" I yelled. Baar, not allowed in the room, stared at me, while Westmayer laughed.

"I thought this was it. Something big that they have to send by encrypted message. Turned out to only be a damned test!"

Days later, on August 2, 1990, at 11 p.m., an alarm sounded. I had never heard an alarm at the depot before, and I really didn't know what to do. I heard a commotion outside in the hallway and opened the door to see soldiers scrambling toward the entrance.

"Everyone report to the admin building on the double!" I rushed out with Merkins, who drove the VW bus to the admin building. We made a formation inside the building, and the company commander was there in full battle gear. Hooker was on staff duty that night and stood at the office entrance. We stood in formation, a mish mash of t-shirts, BDU pants and flip flops. The company commander began to speak.

"At 2:00am, local Kuwaiti time, the country of Iraq launched a full-scale invasion of the Kingdom of Kuwait. The United States is determined to help its ally and is making preparations to defend the kingdom.

"From this point, the depot is on lockdown. The main gate will be manned at all times by military police, who will be aiding the German gate guards. IDs will be checked every time someone enters the depot, and a sign in sheet will be present in the guard shack for non-military civilians. Also, for the next week, no foreign nationals will be admitted to the depot. I will be posting assignment options in the HQ building as they come up. That is all."

We jumped to attention as she left. Everyone slowly started to leave, and I went into the staff office.

"Dammit, Hooker. You got that EAM, didn't you?"

He grinned at me.

"The Iraqis couldn't invade another country on the day I had staff duty? They had to wait until Hooker was on duty, didn't they?"

"You know it." He smiled again.

Life went on as normal, with just a few inconveniences. Our German friends now had to sign in at the main gate, under the watchful eyes of MPs in Humvees and sitting in gun turrets with M60s trained at the entrance. Germans could no longer stay overnight when we had parties, but we ignored that rule, knowing the gate guards would not come looking for them.

Desert Shield began to ramp up, and more soldiers were deployed to Saudi Arabia. Since we were not in a combat arms or logistics MOS, and the United States was not deploying tactical nuclear warheads, I doubted that any 55Gs would be sent there.

In the following weeks orders started to come down, and some of the soldiers in the 64th Ordnance Company and the 165th Military Police Company were called to the desert. I watched them, truck drivers and MPs, pack their belongings for deployment.

I asked Sergeant Kilgens the next day how I could deploy to Saudi Arabia. This was the reason I signed up, and I thought of my father sweating and bleeding in Vietnam back in the late 1960s.

"I want to go, sergeant," I begged. "I need to go," I told him. I knew I had to go to Kilgens; he was also a Vietnam vet and was awarded a Bronze Star and Purple Heart. He looked very impressive in his Class A uniform, all decked out in ribbons and campaign badges. I used to go with him, calling his five rows of ribbons a "fruit salad," and he told me to shut the hell up, that I didn't know anything and was a smart-ass. Truth was, I respected the man very much and yearned for his approval.

Begging Sergeant Kilgens paid off; he said he would see what he could do.

I put in for a 30-day leave, which was granted. I hoped that when I returned, I would have an answer about deploying to the Persian Gulf.

I first took a bus to Pirmasens and then a transfer bus to Ramstein Air Base. I arrived mid-afternoon and got to the ticket counter to put my name in for a standby ticket. Flying standby only cost $10, no matter where in the world a military member wanted to fly. I found a spot against the wall and put down my duffle bag, using it as a pillow. A few hours later, my name was called. There was a flight to Scott Air Force

5. Familiar Faces

Base, just outside St. Louis. I paid the $10 and jumped on a C5 Galaxy, the largest aircraft I had ever seen.

On board, there were only ten rows of seats, and the windowless fuselage gave me an odd feeling of claustrophobia. The passengers were all given earplugs and a brown bag lunch.

The aircraft lifted off, and I was forced to put in my earplugs, which I wanted to avoid. The engines were deafening, and the earplugs barely muffled the sound. The flight took about ten hours, and I was happy when we deboard the flying monstrosity. From Scott Air Force Base, I took a taxi to St. Louis and caught a plane to Chicago's Midway International Airport.

My family was home when I arrived and completely overjoyed to see me. I hugged them all in sequence, from my father to my youngest brother, who was 11 years old. I had not seen my father since Christmas of 1989, and I noticed that he was stressed about something. I sat down on the couch, which was in the same spot as when I left. I opened a beer that my father offered me and put it down on the same end table that was also there when I left. As we talked and drank, I zoned out and look around the house. Same wall colors, same carpeting, even the TV is in the same spot. My brothers all have the same haircuts, and the kitchen still has the same blue wall phone as when I left.

I took notice of all this and realized that nothing has changed since I left. My father asked me questions, and I just nodded at them, half paying attention. Within my first hour of being home, I was ready to go back to Germany.

The next day was busy, as I visited relatives, hopping from one to another. I also tried to visit as many friends as possible. There was a festival going on in Brookfield and we decided to go there. I took a seat in the beer tent, where I saw more people from the neighborhood drinking beer and having a good time. They had to have older people buy the beer for them, and, forgetting where I was, I walked up to the beer table and asked for a beer.

"I need to see your I.D.," the small, red-haired lady said. I produced my military ID and handed it to her.

She looked at the I.D., which was green and had a photo of me with a bald head and a black eye I got the night before I left for MEPS, after getting in a fight at a gas station.

She stared at the I.D. like it was a passport from Mars.

"Don't you have an Illinois driver's license?" I shook my head no. "Sorry, honey, no alcohol." I walked back to the table in anger, feeling defeated. I ended up taking gulps from other people's beer, until I found an "adult" to buy one for me.

At the table, everyone bombarded me with questions, and even started to hack on me, calling me "G.I. Joe" and "soldier boy." I took it all in, not angry, but frustrated at being the target of their jokes.

"Hey, Jeff!" a voice called out to me. I turned around and saw the owner of the engine shop where I worked when I enlisted sitting at a table with some older men. I walked over, shook his dry and calloused hand, and took a seat with him and his friends.

"What division are you in?" asked my former boss.

"Uh, I'm not in a division, I'm with the 64th Ordnance Company." I got confused stares from the men at the table. They must have assumed that I was an infantryman.

"I work on nukes," I told them, which caused some oohs and aahs. After listening to me explain for few minutes what I do, they lost interest. I think they wanted some tales from the field, which I could not supply. I excused myself from the table and went back to my friends. We finished the night drunk and eating burritos at a restaurant in Summit, Illinois.

My grandparents were ecstatic to see me. They also questioned me about Europe, if it had changed since they visited me last year. They also asked about Georg and his family. I told them everyone was well, and things were the same as before. I had dinner with them that night and took in the Old World atmosphere that always permeated their house.

My great-grandfather built the house, and it had been in the family ever since. My grandmother had her wedding reception in the basement, and both of my great-grandparents passed away on the first floor. When my brothers and I were children, we gathered there on Sundays, with the older Croatian men drinking beer and playing pinochle in the kitchen, while we sat in the living room with my great-grandmother and the women.

I appreciated my grandparents because they understood European culture and tried to keep parts of it alive for the next generation of family members.

The rest of my leave was spent going to parties and meeting old

5. Familiar Faces

friends. The time flew by, and I soon found myself flying back to Germany.

When I got back to the depot after my 30-day leave, it was back to business as usual. We had another weapons qualification, but this time it was held at a small range on the depot. We had ammo that needed to be expended, and we also needed to qualify for night fire. We got to the range at dusk, just as the MPs were finishing qualifying with the M249 SAW (Squad Automatic Weapon). They were smaller than the M60 I am used to and easier to handle.

After the MPs cleared the range, darkness settled in and we took positions in our lanes. The rangemaster had the brilliant idea to hang glow sticks from the top of the silhouettes and calling it nightfire.

"Do not fire at the glow sticks!" he yelled. I turned my head and looked at Merkins in the next lane. He nodded at me, smiling.

Even though I was right handed, I fired weapons lefty. I had to clip a round deflector onto the ejection port of my M16 to stop expended rounds from hitting me in the face. I lay there and slapped the 20-round magazine into the weapon when ordered to. We were to expend the magazine, then laid the M16 on its side in the dirt, so the rangemaster knew it was empty.

"Commence firing!" he yelled. I took my time and slowly squeezed the trigger, trying to hit a target I couldn't see. The glow sticks only illuminated so far, and the soft green glow did little to light up the target. I squeezed off ten rounds, then turned to look at Merkins. He smiled, then shot ... and hit the glow stock. The glow stick exploded, and green goo splattered all over the target. I followed suit, squeezed the trigger, and missed. I tried again and again, and on the seventh round, I finally hit it: *splat*. As if on cue, the other lanes started firing at the glow sticks, and by the time the rangemaster was yelling, "*Ceasefire! Ceasefire!*" it was too late. The targets were covered in green liquid. He started cussing up a storm, and we stood and moved away from the lanes as commanded.

Merkins started to laugh hard, sounding exactly like Roger from the television show *What's Happening!!* This made the rangemaster even angrier, and for retaliation, he made Merkins remove the targets and hang new ones up, complete with neon red glow sticks. After the weapons were cleared, we moved out from the range, as Bravo platoon took its positions. We sat on some bleachers and watched as they began firing. All went well at first, then *splat*, a red glow stick exploded. The hint taken, the other shooters began firing until all the targets were covered in red slime.

The following day, our platoon began required field training, which we were not used to. In the forest south of Area One, we dug foxholes in the soft sandy ground and eat MREs. Sergeant Kilgens went over platoon tactics, using the knowledge he gained in Vietnam in addition to published tactics NCOs learn at BNOC (Basic Noncommissioned Officer Course). Being the M60 gunner, I carried the weapon as if on patrol, with Thomkins as my assistant gunner. Each squad also had a M203 grenadier. The M203 was a grenade attachment to the M16 which launched 40-mm grenades. Each squad also had one automatic rifleman who kept his weapon on the automatic setting while the remaining squad members kept their selectors at semi-automatic.

We moved silently into the forest, with Sergeant Kilgens on point. This was one part of training I took seriously, and I follow every direction exactly. A couple of hundred meters out, Sergeant Kilgens raised a fist in the air. This was the "stop and get down" signal. We took a knee to the ground. Kilgens then spoke quietly: "We are going to set up an ambush. Squads one and two, begin to form a semicircle on my left flank. Squads three and four, form a semicircle on my right flank, except Woodward, who will be the pivot point at the top of the half circle with the M60."

We formed quickly. I laid on the mossy, wet ground, and Thompkins got down next to me. I saw the others go out of sight, and the forest was completely silent.

Sergeant Kilgens stood in the center of the semicircle. He was smiling, obviously impressed with his platoon. I think sometimes he missed being an 11B, an infantryman. After we sat there for a while, he called us back. "This is a basic wedge ambush. This is for an approaching platoon sized enemy force traveling on a known trail in wooded areas. The M60 is the anchor of the ambush, and firing should not commence until most of the enemy is within the semicircle."

We listened to Sergeant Kilgens, knowing that he was the only one present who had actually been in combat. My respect for the man grew, and I promised myself to pay more attention to the instructions he gave us and to not smart off so often.

We finished the day by playing infantrymen and eating MREs. I

5. Familiar Faces

always ended up with the franks and beans, which I had a hard time stomaching. No one wanted to trade with me, so I threw my MRE into the woods. We'd be back at the barracks in a few hours, and I could eat something there.

I was told that I could not deploy to Saudi Arabia; that really bugged me. Our soldiers who deployed there were attached to the 76th Transportation Company, which was stationed in Kaiserslautern. Maybe if I was a truck driver I could have deployed, but for a nuke tech, the wartime deployment opportunity was nonexistent. Sergeant Kilgens consoled me in his own way, telling me that our mission was just as important. This actually made me feel better, coming from him. I knew that nukes would not be deployed to the Middle East; it would be a political and a humanitarian nightmare. Being involved in a politically sensitive MOS did have its pitfalls.

I spent the rest of the night drinking in the EM club, partying with the usual suspects who frequented it on a nightly basis. I succumbed to boredom and saw myself drinking almost nightly. Chief Boyd mentioned to me that I should slow down, but I used the alcohol to help ease the homesickness, boredom and nightmares that had been plaguing me.

We got short notice that the 59th Ordnance Brigade commander would be arriving for an inspection of the depot. We scrambled to clean the barracks, police the outside of trash and cigarette butts, and get our Class As ready. I had recently been promoted to private first class and had just picked up my uniform, with my new rank patch, from the dry cleaners.

When the commander showed up, a thunderstorm began, so we were herded to the gym for an in-ranks inspection. We lined up by platoon and waited for him to enter. Everyone was on edge, but Sergeant Kilgens eased the tension by making coy remarks about officers and their lack of real-life experience. His five rows of ribbons, Vietnam campaign badge, and blue cord around his shoulder (the identifier of an infantryman), in addition to his Bronze Star and Purple Heart, made him the most decorated soldier in Fischbach.

The commander briskly entered and we snapped to attention. He stood in front of the company and gave a speech about how well we were doing, how important our mission was the United States and NATO, and his pride in the overall organization of the 59th Ordnance Brigade.

Last of the Glow Worms

After speaking, he began the inspection. He moved through the ranks, nodding and smiling at each soldier he passed. We were the last platoon, and I stood there sweating in my uniform as he took his time maneuvering up and down and left and right.

It seemed like an eternity before he got to the M&A platoon. Naturally, he greeted our platoon leader with a handshake and then approached Sergeant Kilgens. The commander greeted him warmly, shaking his hand and smiling from ear to ear. I saw the commander also had a battle patch and row upon row of ribbons and an expert combat infantry badge. After a few minutes of speaking with Kilgens, he made his way through our ranks. He once again smiled and nodded everyone; he smiled at Hooker, nodded at Merkins, smiled at Thompkins, nodded at Preston ... then stopped in front of me.

I was shaking. The commander looked at me and smiled. He put out his hand, and I took it in a firm handshake. I saw something move out of the corner of my left eye, but I was too afraid to move my head. The general looked at me, then leaned in a little closer.

"You didn't think I would forget about you, Woodward, did you?" he said softly. I was freaking out now, because I had no idea what that meant. He reached in his pocket and pulled out a coin. He once again took my hand, and he put the coin in it.

"Keep up the good work, Woodward," he said with a smile. I saw a flash of light to my left, as his official photographer took a photo.

"Thank you, sir!" I replied, hoping not too loudly. He walked away and finished up the inspection with another speech to the company. Then he left.

As soon as the general left the building, everyone started to file out. I stood there for a second, and my platoon members surrounded me. I knew what they wanted, so I pulled the coin out of my pocket.

I had never seen a challenge coin before. Made of brass, about the size of a silver dollar, it read "The General's Best" on the face, which was also engraved with the 59th Ordnance Brigade unit insignia. The reverse showed a map of Germany, with the various ordnance company location on the map.

Everyone wanted it. Merkins wanted to buy it for $10. Sergeant Kilgens slapped me on the back. We all started to leave the gym, and I began to wonder.

What did the general mean by "I didn't forget you?" Maybe he

5. Familiar Faces

knew something I didn't, or maybe he was just toying with me by using a well-rehearsed line on soldiers who looked nervous.

Hooker and I decided to take a day trip to Luxembourg, a small country northwest of Germany. We jumped in his BMW and began the two-hour drive. I popped a Metallica cassette into the radio and we began singing along to "And Justice for All," headbanging as we maneuvered down Thunder Road to get to Pirmasens and the Autobahn. I reached in my pocket for a cigarette and saw a car approaching slowly. I told Hooker to slow down, and I looked at the license plates. This was a hobby I picked up in Europe, making it a game to identify the first two letters of a German plate to figure out where a car is from or the different colored plates to see which country it is from. For example, the French have yellow license plates and yellow lenses over their headlights.

As this car approached, I could not make out the plate. I told Hooker to slow the car down even more, and I strained to make out the plate. It was yellow and had a small red flag with a large number 6 in black, bold letters.

"Oh crap, it's the Russians!" I shouted.

"What?"

"The Russians! One of those SMLM cars!" The car started to pass us, and I saw two men inside it, wearing military uniforms. They were both clean-shaven and they looked at us quickly before speeding up.

"Dude, you have to turn around! We have to follow them!"

"For what?" responded Hooker, shrugging his shoulders. "What are we going to do? C'mon, man, forget about them. Let's go."

I was in a strange mood the rest of the trip. Luxembourg City was beautiful, and we enjoyed drinks at an outdoor cafe. But all I could think about was the Russians so close to our depot. Hooker was right; what the hell were we going to do about it? We had no weapons and there was no phone in the vicinity. I didn't know what number to call anyway. I let the whole situation drop and tried to enjoy the rest of the trip, which involved Hooker flexing his biceps in front of monuments while I snapped the photos of him doing it.

6

Culture Shock

I was happy that I chose Germany over the other stations of choice when I first enlisted, and I was doubly happy that I was sent to the Pirmasens.

Americans have had a presence in the area since after World War II. We were part of the Pirmasens Military Community, which paled in size to the Kaiserslautern Military Community just north of Pirmasens. The Kaiserslautern Military Community was home to more than 50,000 military personnel, their families and civilian contractors, and was where we would travel if we wanted the newest American products from the PX or to hit up American-style fast food joints like Pizza Hut or Kentucky Fried Chicken.

The depot being an isolated installation, we needed to find ways to entertain ourselves, which usually meant drinking and going to discos. The Germans in the area held something called the "Rolling Disco Show," a traveling disco that took place in different surrounding towns every weekend. On Friday, it might be in Bruechweiler, and on Saturday, it might be in Hauenstein. This was where I meet most of my German friends, including Georg, who quickly became a good friend and party pal.

We were on relatively good terms with the surrounding community, and many Americans had German girlfriends. At the local festivals, it was not uncommon to see Americans and Germans sitting together, drinking from one-liter beer steins and singing German songs.

We attended other festivals, most notably one at Castle Dahn, the castle walls and turrets swarming with Germans and American soldiers. Everyone took part in the festivities, drinking beer and dancing to the music was supplied by a DJ.

I was with Hooker and a truck driver named Sutherland. We were partying it up, trying to out-drink the Germans, which wasn't a very good idea. They were used to the higher percentage of alcohol in their beer, while we were used to what they called "pisswater."

The game began, and we started chugging one-liter steins of beer. I couldn't keep up, and after the first liter of beer, I was toast. I dropped out and sat down, my back against the castle wall, my head spinning like a tilt-a-whirl.

Hooker tried to keep up, but he soon dropped out too, much to the humor of the Germans. He came and plopped down next to me, and we tried watching the rest of the contest with blurred vision.

I gave Sutherland credit for lasting as long as he did. He eventually fell out, wobbly legs making him stumble and eventually fall. The Germans laughed and toasted us.

Sutherland, not to be outdone, climbed on top of a smaller parapet that stood 15 feet high. He balanced himself on the ledge and shouted, "Look out!" before jumping off the ledge. He landed feet first, and his legs buckled, causing his face to slam into the hard dirt.

A crowd began to swarm around him, Germans and Americans alike, to look at the motionless soldier lying on the ground. No one moved, and the crowd stood quiet in silent anticipation. Suddenly, Sutherland jumped up. He raised his arms in the air as a sign of victory, ignorant to the fact that his face was a bloody mess. He smiled at the crowds with outstretched arms, showing the chip that took half of his upper front tooth.

I hung around with Sutherland regularly, to the dismay and annoyance of Chief Vega. Sutherland was a truck driver, 88M. He liked to drink, and we had numerous parties in his barracks room, blasting thrash music and death metal. The room would be packed with soldiers, drunk and slam dancing into each other.

Sutherland had a German girlfriend who lived in an apartment row behind my girlfriend's apartment building. She had two children from previous relationships, one of them with an American soldier. Sutherland would spend the weekend with her, enjoying home cooked meals and a civilian bed.

His girlfriend became pregnant two weeks before his PCS date. I was present when she told him, and being the carefree guy that he was, he told her that everything would be okay and he would take care of the child. The United States and Germany had an international agreement concerning custodial and child support rights for German mothers of American children. I pulled Sutherland aside to tell him this, and he brushed it off. When she asked him his address back in the States, he told her, "1034 Audubon Drive, Memphis, Tennessee." I looked at him, knowing that he was from the southwest. He chuckled and wrote the address down on a piece of paper for her. After dinner at her apartment, we left. While walking down the street, I asked him whose address that was he gave her.

"Graceland, son," he responded with a hearty laugh. "That's Elvis' address."

Every once in a while we would go to a very small punk club, whose entrance was located beneath some stairs on the *Fussgängerzone* in Pirmasens. It was called the Jugendhaus and was basically off-limits to Americans, since soldiers were not allowed to enter. I chanced upon it with Sutherland and another soldier one night. Needing a new place to go, I walked to the door, which was locked from the inside. I banged on the door, and a small peephole slid open. Music was playing from inside, so I know it was open.

"Lass uns rein!" I said to the person behind the door. The eyes started at us for a moment and then the peephole slid shut. I heard a fumbling with the lock, and the door opened.

The club was dark, and the Dead Kennedys were playing in the background. Sutherland and the other guy got a table in the back while I went to the bar to get beer. There were a few people there, and the Germans at the bar were sporting blue Mohawks. The girl behind the bar was very pretty and had one side of her head shaved while on the other side she had very long hair tipped with red highlights. She smiled and gave me our beer, which I brought back to the table.

After chugging the beer, we decided to hit the dance floor. Sutherland started to move, then suddenly slammed into me, almost knocking me down. I retaliated by shoving him and then shoving the other guy. We were moving in a circle on the dance floor, knocking each other around to the music of the Exploited. The Germans at the bar got up and came out to join us. In moments, Germans and Americans were slam dancing on the floor, only stopping to take a swig of beer. The intensity of it all had me reeling, until I couldn't move anymore.

We end up sitting at the bar with the Germans, who opened up and told us they didn't like Americans, but "you guys are okay." They

6. Culture Shock

saw Americans as occupiers who took German women and acted like brutes in public. Americans demanded that everyone speak English to them and made no efforts to learn about the German culture.

I agreed on some points, but also pointed out that most Americans don't ask to come to Germany, that it is a requirement to be stationed overseas at least once during their military careers. Some have difficulty adjusting and just want to do their time and go home. I have European relatives, which makes it a little easier for me than for others who have had no contact with people outside of America.

I also told him that we have the same taste in music and girls, by the looks of things. He laughed and bought me a shot of Jack Daniels.

Sutherland and the other guy were trying to talk to the bartender, who was rebuking their advances. They didn't speak German, but they tried to talk to her with the few phrases they learned during orientation. I told her to ignore them, which I guess didn't need saying, because she was doing a great job at keeping them at a distance.

By the end of the night, we got an invitation to come back the next weekend. This was an early lesson for me in German-American relations.

On Thursday nights we would go to a small dance club in Niederschlettenbach, about ten miles from Fischbach. If no car was available, we would hitchhike, then worry about getting back to depot later. Germans would pick us up, and since Hooker or Merkins had no grasp of German, I would do the talking.

The club was small in comparison to the clubs in Pirmasens. It had a counter at the entrance, and booths lined up, allowing a path to the rear of the building. In the rear were the restrooms to the right, and another bar to the left, where the Germans mostly hang out. There was is a small dance floor located in the center of the club. Americans would dance with their German girlfriends, while the German men mostly stayed at the bar drinking beer and shots of Asbach. If the club got too smoky, we went outside to hang out in front of the entrance, greeting friends as they entered.

After the club closed, we would either try to hitch a ride home or call the staff office on depot and ask for the staff duty driver to come get us. Technically this was a no-no, but since my platoon performed staff duty, we usually got the ride after a round of pleading with whoever was on duty. The exception was if Sergeant Kilgens was on duty. He would tell me to find my own way home and hang up.

The town of Bobenthal was just to the south of Niederschettenbach. We went there to visit the tomb of Hans von Trotha, a famous 14th-century knight. The tomb was located along the side of the road, and we tried to gain access to it, but the tomb was locked.

In 1485, during a dispute with the abbot of Wissembourg, Hans had the Wieslauter River dammed in Bobenthal to prevent water from reaching the town of Wissembourg, denying residents a water supply. The abbot, in a frenzy because the town was running out of fresh water, tried to make peace with von Trotha. Hans agreed to open the dam and broke it open. The resulting flood of water devastated Wissembourg, ruining the town's economy.

When we wanted more excitement, we took the bus to Pirmasens. The city had a *Fussgängerzone*, which was a pedestrian-only street with boutiques and cafes. To more fully immerse myself in the culture, I would often frequent places that the Americans avoided, for example, small punk clubs and cafes run by non–Germans. I found a small cafe owned by Yugoslavians, who were Bosnian. After I frequented the cafe for a few weeks, we started talking, and I told them my mother was Croatian. The were jubilant at first, but when they realized my Croatian language skills were almost nonexistent, they quickly fell suspicious. I had to explain, over piping hot espressos, that in America, immigrants want their children to learn English as a first language, so many times the parents' mother tongue becomes lost. They seemed to accept this explanation, and the issue was dropped.

The Germans in the Palatinate speak a dialect called *Pfälzisch*, which was very different from the High German taught in high school and college. I took three years of German in high school, and I can hold a conversation on a basic level. The locals in the area could tell right away that I was an American or Brit. Our consonant "r" is vocalized much harder than in German, as they speak it softly, just as a Bostonian in America would. An ethnic slur against Americans in Germany was "*Kaugummiknatscher*," which translates roughly as "one who chews gum loudly." This was due to the way that Americans pronounced German words.

Pfälzisch was also is distinct from High German, with some loanwords from French and English. The Amish in America speak a dialect of Pfälzisch, as they originated from this region.

It was not uncommon for Germans from different regions of the

6. Culture Shock

country to have small troubles understanding each other. My friend Georg would speak the dialect and mix it with slang words to confuse me. After a while, I picked up on them, and started using them myself, much to the amusement of my German friends.

With its rolling hills and thick forests, the Palatinate was also home to many castles in various states of disrepair.

The nearest castle was in Dahn, called Dahnfels. Dahnfels sat on top of a small hill, and its brick and sandstone walls were in ruins. Whenever we would climb to the top of the rampart, I would imagine myself as a knight, preparing for battle against a neighboring kingdom. Standing at the top of the castle walls, I could see the *Jungfrausprung*, which is a cliff high above the town and marked by a large steel cross. Legend has it that a maiden was chased up the hill by a knight, who wanted to ravish her. The two varying accounts are she leaped from the cliff to her death to avoid being dishonored, or that she jumped from the cliff and her dress caught the wind, allowing her to float safely to the ground.

Visiting castles became a pastime that I enjoyed. The most famous I visited was Castle Trifels, located in the town of Annweiler. Built in 1081, the castle was famous for holding Richard the Lionheart, King of England, captive for three weeks during his return from the Third Crusade.

Other areas of interest included the Maginot Line, a line of defense erected by the French on the border with Germany before World War II. I went there with Hooker and took a tour through the underground tunnels, marveling at the defense works. Highlighting the end of the tour was an American Sherman Tank, left there by Patton's 3rd Division.

Every once in awhile, we would hang out in France, trying different bars and clubs. The perception of Americans in France was different than in Germany. The French seemed more stand-offish, and I can only contribute that to pride. When sitting in a bar, Hooker and I would be the only Americans, and since we didn't speak French, we would have to order in English or German. Since this area was part of Germany at one time, many of the older citizens spoke German, while the younger generation either avoided it or never learned it. The bartender would put the drinks on the counter and pretend he was busy cleaning glasses or watching TV. There would be no small talk, and I tried hard to understand the barriers between us. I was not very political, but I knew there was a rift between our countries after Charles de Gaulle took office and pushed for French influence worldwide. This included pulling France out of NATO and demanding American troops stationed in France to leave.

The French may have had a love-hate relationship with America, but there was no denying that their taste in food was spectacular. One regional dish that was popular in both the Alsace and the Palatinate is *tarte flambe* (known as *Flammkuchen* in German), bread dough rolled out very thinly, covered with white cheese, onions and bacon, baked in a wood-burning oven at a high temperature. This quickly became a favorite of mine.

Every now and then I talked someone into going to Kaiserslautern, which had the largest concentration of American soldiers in the world outside of CONUS. Because it was so large, every amenity catering to Americans was available. One weekend we drove there to try a "Chicago-style" pizza restaurant just outside of the city. Since Hooker was stationed at Fort Sheridan, he volunteered to go with us, to give it a taste test. I reminded him that I was the only legitimate Chicagoan in the car, and I would be the judge of the authenticity of the pizza. I made sure to bring Merkins along, since he had an appetite on par with a sasquatch.

We drove about an hour to get there, our stomachs growling with hunger. We sat down and ordered some beers. The restaurant was decked out in gangster memorabilia; photos of Al Capone, Frank Nitti, crime scenes and Tommy guns hung on the walls, which I found rather tacky. It was bad enough telling a German you were from Chicago and hearing him or her automatically say, "Al Capone, bang-bang." Now I had to see it hanging on the walls at a pizza joint.

"Two large, deep dish pizzas, one with sausage, and the other plain cheese," I told the server. She nodded and went to the kitchen with our order.

"Now Merkins," I began. "I know y'all are used to cardboard style pizza with that nasty breakfast sausage on it instead of Italian sausage, so you better be prepared for heaven." Merkins laughed at my jab, but knew that I was right.

Twenty minutes later, our pizzas arrived. I rubbed my hands together with delight when I saw the two-inch-thick pie with pizza sauce covering the top. Steam rose from the sauce, and the aroma reminded me of home.

I gave slices to Hooker and Merkins, then finally set one onto my plate. Chicago-style pizzas need a fork and knife to be eaten, and I slowly cut into my piece, starting at the crust. The crust is where you can tell how good a pizza is going to taste. I sliced off a piece of the golden crust and put it into my mouth. The taste was there, crusty on the outside, but soft and chewy on the inside. It passed the test.

Next, I moved to the other side of the piece of pizza and tried the sauce and cheese. The sauce was tart yet sweet, but had too much oregano in it. The cheese was typical mozzarella. They were just as good as any pizza I had in Chicago.

I then tried the sausage. I chewed on it a bit, trying to figure out the flavor. It definitely was not Italian sausage. Then it hit me. Germany. Bratwurst. A logical combination.

I watched as Merkins and Hooker tried to finish both of the pizzas. I was bursting at the seams after two pieces, but these two had almost eaten enough to feed six people.

When the pizzas were finished, only crumbs were left. I asked Hooker if he enjoyed them. He gave me a thumbs up, unable to speak in fear of the pizza coming back up.

"And you, Merkins?"

"It was awesome! All except the sausage. It tasted funny."

Kaiserslautern also had many dance clubs, but I avoided them because too many Americans were there. I would just walk the *Fussgängerzone* in search of new places to discover. Most of the stores were American-driven, and you could tell that the local economy depended on American dollars just as much as it depended on German marks.

With the reunification of East and West Germany, the Soviet threat began to diminish, though we were still at a heightened state of alert due to the events in the Persian Gulf. The Russians began to withdraw from the former Warsaw Pact countries, leaving only small garrisons in place until full independence was achieved by each nation.

Even terrorist threats from organizations such as the RAF (Red Army Faction) began to fade. The RAF was a far-left terrorist group which had committed acts of terror in Kaiserslautern and detonated a car bomb at the Ramstein Air Force Base in 1981. The proximity of these attacks led me to believe that the RAF or similar organizations were watching the depot, trying to figure out ways to attack it or cause damage. I was fairly certain that there were Germans sympathetic to their cause, and I took extra precautions to avoid answering questions pertaining to the operations at the depot.

The questions inevitably arose when we were out, at a disco or somewhere else. The Germans were curious about what was happening inside of the fence, and I was sure many of them had been to the Eye of Ludwigswinkel and looked down into Area One.

The 41st Ordnance Detachment worked with missile sections, which required a large, clear area due to the volatility of the rocket propellant. The Germans began to mistake the 41st as a chemical weapons unit, and when word began to spread, the protests began.

Georg even asked about Area One. He told me that he was certain there was nerve gas there; he heard it from a friend whose relative was once a gate guard in Fischbach and saw the canisters enter by truck. I fumbled for words and told him that I had never seen poison gas there and I had no idea what went on in Area One. I couldn't use the "I clean toilets" line on Georg; he was too intelligent to buy that nonsense. I stuck with the "I don't know" answers until he dropped the subject.

Hanging out with Georg, I got a deeper glimpse into German culture. I learned that it was impolite to not eat every piece of food on your plate when invited to dinner, that when someone offered you a gift, you took it without question and said, "Thank you," and that when somebody bought you a drink at a bar, there was no obligation to return the favor. You just bought him one the next time you went out with him.

Georg had a taste for anything American, and I used my ration card to purchase Jack Daniels and chewing tobacco as gifts for him. When he told me how much Jack Daniels cost on the German market compared to the PX prices, I found a lucrative way to make extra cash. I filled up my ration card quickly, purchasing cartons of Marlboro cigarettes and hard liquor, which I sold to the Germans at double the price. I had to use Hooker's ration card when mine filled up, and I cut him in on the profits.

Though relations were cordial between the Americans and local nationals, there were some Germans that did not want us there. We would see stickers on road signs reading, "*Ami Go Home!*" (ami was a shortened version of "American" used by the Germans). I think these

6. Culture Shock

were put up by the Greens, who had been advocating the removal of U.S. troops from German soil for years.

Now, with East and West Germany unified, right-wing militant groups were on the rise in western Germany. Skinheads, who had little to no presence in the Pirmasens area before 1989, had been popping up with more frequency since unification. They had not made any threats to any American military personnel as far as I knew and tended to focus their politics on foreigners, such as Turks and Arabs.

Sometimes while driving in a military vehicle through town, someone would give us the middle finger, which I found humorous. I would just wave, while Hooker or Merkins would get mad and give him the finger right back.

There were some Americans that had negative views of the Germans and did not attempt to socialize with them. Those soldiers usually stayed on depot or hung out exclusively with other Americans. They took guided tours to the Alps or to the Black Forest, but always with other Americans. I did not understand their mentality, nor did I try to change their opinion of the host country's inhabitants. I felt that they were missing out on the culture around them and were just biding their time until they were rotated back to the United States.

In addition to Americans in Germany, there were also Brits and Canadians. Some British soldiers came to Fischbach for training. I met some of them at the EM club, and we began buying shots for each other. We were laughing and having a good time, sharing stories, either true or made up, about our military experiences. During the laughter, a ruckus broke out in the back room of the club. There were some slot machines back there, and a Brit was playing one, losing his money. He was very drunk, and in a rage he began yanking on the slot machine's arm, trying to break it off. Some of the other British soldiers were egging him on, yelling his name as he pulled the machine from the wall. The Americans sat there, either amused by the show, or too drunk to care. Eventually, a British NCO came in and ended the scene by grabbing the soldier and yelling at him to cool down.

There was very little interaction between our company and the German military, although I would have liked to work with them if I'd had the chance. There was a special medal that could be earned by American soldiers who qualified with German weapons called the *Schuetzenschnur.* The qualification consisted of shooting three different type of German weapons: the G36 Rifle, the P8 Pistol and the MG3 Machine Gun. If successful, an American enlisted soldier could wear the decoration on his Class A Uniform, one of only a few foreign decorations allowed by the United States military.

In the city of Bitsche, France, 23 miles to the west of Fischbach, there was a French Foreign Legion recruitment center. I had met some of the Legionnaires one Thursday night at the club in Niederschlettenbach. They were sitting at a table with the Germans we knew, and I sat down next to them. After they introduced themselves, I told them I was in the U.S. Army. They seemed intrigued and asked what my job was. I decided not to go with the usual "I clean toilets" routine and told them I worked with rockets. They responded by saying they were infantry. Both were speaking German, but I noticed that they spoke with accents. I prodded them, and they admitted that they were Tunisians, which opened a can worms; much to their dismay, I spent the rest of the night asking them about Tunisia and its culture. Buying them rounds of drinks also helped loosen their tongues, and they opened up about their perspective of Americans, which was mostly negative. I tried to dispel their prejudice by being as polite as possible. By the end of the night, we were all like old friends, and I hoped that they would take a second look at the views of Americans.

I got the itch to travel again, and I tried to find a partner to go with me to Frankfurt for a day trip. All the regular guys were busy, but I found a suitable travel companion in a soldier named Reyes. I had partied with him before at the EM club, and he seemed all right. We took the bus to Pirmasens and walked to the train station. From there, we took the train to Kaiserslautern and purchased tickets to Frankfurt and a bottle of Apfelkorn (a sweet, apple-flavored liqueur). We began drinking as soon as the train left the station, and soon I was very tipsy. Feeling tired, I fell asleep.

I felt a tap on my shoulder, and I woke up groggily. A conductor was looking at me, and he asked for my ID in German. I told him I didn't have one and showed him my military ID. He looked at it, and I asked him how much longer to Frankfurt. He looked at me quizzically and told me that the train left Frankfurt station two hours ago. Confused, I kicked at Reyes to wake up, and he angrily asked what was going on. I looked out of the train window, and the first thing I noticed was that the buildings were rundown and decrepit. I began to freak out; there

6. Culture Shock

was something wrong here. I told him to look, and he also noticed something wasn't right.

After a few minutes of anxiety, we pulled into a large train station. We disembarked and we saw the sign: ERFURT.

I had no idea exactly where the city of Erfurt was in relation to Germany as a whole, but I began to realize quickly that it was in eastern Germany.

We left the train station and started to walk aimlessly down the street. Trabis, small East German cars with two cylinders and a plastic chassis, drove down the street blowing smoke. The buildings were old and looked like they hadn't been repaired in decades.

Since we were there, we decided to stop at the nearest bar. The establishment was empty, except for the bartender and an old man sitting at a table near the window. We ordered beer, and I handed the bartender a 100-dollar bill. He looked at it, then said, *"Ihr seid Amerikaner?"*

"Ja," I responded in German. "We are Americans." He smiled and handed the bill back. "You are the first Americans to visit my business. This drink is free." I reached my hand out, and he took it firmly. He was a huge man, and I tried not to wince under the pressure of the handshake. I explained to him what had happened to us, and he almost couldn't believe it. I told him it was true, and he laughed heartily, his belly bouncing up and down.

We left the bar to catch a train back to Kaiserslautern. On the street we passed some soldiers wearing solid olive green uniforms and high leather jack boots. I couldn't tell of they were German or Soviet soldiers, since the Russians still had a small presence here in eastern Germany. I refrained from asking them, not wanting to possibly start an incident. We purchased our tickets back to Kaiserslautern and forgot about Frankfurt altogether.

A few days later I got a letter from my grandmother. She wrote that my cousin, who was Canadian, was studying banking in Nice, France. She also sent me my cousin's phone number.

I had not seen this cousin since I was a kid, when we traveled to Toronto to visit. These cousins were also Croatians but had settled in Canada instead of the United States. I dialed her number from a pay phone outside of the barracks, and she picked up. We reminisced for a while, and then began talking about current events, including what was happening in Iraq. Before hanging up, I promised to visit her in Nice. She responded by saying that would not be a good idea; Americans were not very well liked there, and tensions had been rising with the local Arab community. I told her to let me know as soon as things calmed down, and I would come to visit her in France.

Since the depot had been on heightened alert, we had been going more often to visit German friends, instead of having them come to the depot to hang us with us. The exception was Georg, who still came to the depot regularly. He introduced me to more of the German culture, and even invited me to his house for Thanksgiving.

Though Germans didn't celebrate the American holiday, Georg still wanted to have a dinner at his house. Another soldier that was stationed with us, Kaminsky, was invited too. I picked up a turkey at the PX, and all the sides, including sweet potatoes, cranberry sauce, and stuffing. Sweet potatoes were not native to Europe, and I could tell the family fell in love with them at the first taste. We drank one-liter steins of beer with dinner, and I began to bond more closely with Georg's family, dispelling the myths about American carelessness and lack of discipline. I understood that some Germans still viewed us as an occupying army, and many American soldiers acted as such, but I wanted to project a positive image of the American soldier, especially since I was stationed at place where, Germans believed, chemical weapons were stored.

Even though it was technically still winter, I traveled with Hooker to Amsterdam to spend a weekend. The city was a four-hour drive from Fischbach, passing through Luxembourg and Belgium along the way. We decided to stop at Brussels and took a small self-guided tour through the city before ending up at a dance-cafe called Calloways.

I was an introvert by nature, so Hooker took the lead in mingling and talking to complete strangers. We ended up at a booth with some girls, who, to Hooker's delight, were Danish. He hit it off well with one of them, and they disappeared, leaving me alone at the table with the other Dane who obviously had no interest in me. After waiting for 45 minutes, I excused myself from the table and walked back to the car. I waited inside, curling up in the backseat before falling asleep.

A few hours later, Hooker reappeared, a broad smile on his face. He started the car, and we started driving to Amsterdam. The whole ride, he bragged about his conquest of the Danish girl. I shut him out and focused on the trip.

6. Culture Shock

Amsterdam was everything I thought it would be. The city was carved into sections by the canals running through it, and the buildings were quaint and very well maintained. Tourists were everywhere, and a hundred languages could be heard as we walk down the street.

There were coffee shops selling marijuana and hashish, brothels marked by neon red signs, and homeless people panhandling for coins.

We jumped from bar to bar, and Hooker made friends with whomever he spoke with. The Dutch were friendly and seemed to have a more favorable view of Americans than Germans or the French. We ended up at a bar with women scantily clad serving drinks. We ordered vodka shots, and the lady serving us smiled and sat down at our table.

"Are you Americans or British?" she asked. I didn't know where this was going, because I was sure that thousands of Americans and Brits must have visited this bar in the past.

"Americans," I responded, with Hooker adding, "We're in the army."

"Oh," she said. "I am from Russia."

Even though I came from Chicago, a multi-ethnic city, I had until this point never met a Russian. She was tall, had raven hair, and had exotic features that we had only seen in movies.

"We are afraid of you," she blurted out. I sat there tipsy and confused at the statement.

"Why's that? There's no reason to be afraid of Americans," I responded, a bit agitated. I did not come to Holland to end up in a political argument with a Russian woman I had just met.

"Our country has fallen apart," she replied to me. "We have nothing. Now America is the power. Maybe I should go there, yes?"

"Yes. Go there."

I told good luck and paid her for the drinks.

We stayed up all night, and since Amsterdam was a 24-hour city, there was no lack of people to meet or bars to visit through the night hours. The people were very friendly, and I quickly fell in love with Holland.

The last tour I took with Hooker was the "Three-Country Bus Tour." This was a quick, 24-hour tour, visiting Switzerland, Liechtenstein and Austria. We began in Pirmasens and drove south to Switzerland first. We passed through the Alps and visited the city of Lucerne. We took photos (Hooker flexing in front of a statue), grabbed a quick bite to eat, and then jumped back on the bus.

The next stop was Leichtenstein, the smallest country in Europe. It covered barely 60 square miles and was sandwiched between Switzerland and Austria. We visited the capital, Vaduz, and marveled at the Alps surrounding it. We stayed for a couple of hours, and the bus left for the final destination, Salzburg, Austria.

The baroque-style buildings of Salzburg were worth with the trip alone. They were gigantic and wondrous, and I disregarded Hooker, who wanted to meet people, to stare at the architecture. The mountains were just to the south of the Salzburg and were a beautiful backdrop to the city. To my dismay, I ran out of film for my camera and did not have enough time to find a store that sold film.

The tour over, we sped back to Pirmasens, racing through Bavaria and the Black Forest, to arrive in Pirmasens in the morning. My eyes were burning from staying up all night, and all I could think about was rest.

Lying in my barracks bunk, I thought of the seven countries we visited that month. I only wished we had more time; I would have liked to have seen all of Europe, and possibly even scouted a place to stay once my ETS (expiration, term of service) date arrives.

Monday morning we were informed that third and fourth squads would be going TDY to Wuerzburg to maintain trainer weapons there. I had not been TDY to this point, and I was looking forward to visiting a different Army base.

7

Nuke Training and Investigations

The third and fourth squads began to pack for TDY to Wuerzburg. We took a stencil machine, radiac meters, and our manuals, marked "secret" in bold red letters. I would be driving the Chevy Blazer with the equipment, a soldier named Gage, and Chief Boyd. Hooker would be driving the VW minibus with the rest of the squad personnel.

Gage was armed with an M16, since we were carrying classified material. It seemed rather odd to me, though, that the weapon was unloaded. There was not even a magazine of ammunition in the vehicle. Gage carrying the M16 was just for show, and, I start to think, if the RAF or another radical group attacks, what would we do? Gage could point the M16 at them, but that's it. Not very intelligent to allow classified material to transport without armed protection, in my opinion.

We arrived in Wuerzburg, a city in northern Bavaria. It was home to the U.S. Army's 3rd Infantry Division, which had casernes spread out across southern and western Germany. We were visiting one of the 155-mm artillery batteries to repair and check on its trainer weapons. Since this was an artillery unit, they were working with the M454 and M422 trainer warheads.

When we arrived, we reported to the unit we were visiting. We let them know we were there, dropped off our equipment (minus the manuals), and drove to the gasthaus where we were staying for the week. We each got our own rooms, and I dropped off my belongings and headed downstairs to eat.

We all sat together and ordered schnitzels and fries. I wanted to go out and explore the city, but Chief Boyd told me to stay in for the night. I could explore after work tomorrow.

Last of the Glow Worms

Our rooms were quaint, with typical German furnishings. I rolled out my uniforms onto the spare bed, took a shower and then went to bed. I fought the urge to leave, to explore and check out the bar scene, and sleep took me.

Men in gas masks loaded cannons, and I heard screams. I looked around but couldn't tell where the screams were coming from. The sky was a dark red, and the men in masks kept taking bundles and loading them into the cannons, firing one after another. I started to walk closer, slowly, and I saw one of the bundles move. A muffled cry came from it as it was heaved up by a masked man and shoved brutally into the cannon. I yelled out, "Stop!" and the man turned in my direction. I couldn't tell if he was looking at me directly, and I started to shrink back as he moved forward. The other masked men also moved forward, with one carrying an empty burlap bag. I began to walk quickly backwards and tripped over a skull. One of them reached down to grab me...

I woke up, frightened, but aware that it was only a dream. I decided to stay awake and take a shower.

After I read for an hour, I heard a knock at my door. I opened it to see Hooker standing there.

"You ready?"

"Yeah, let's go." I went downstairs, where Hooker and I were the first to breakfast. I made a small sandwich with ham and Swiss cheese, while Hooker ate a soft-boiled egg. The rest of the crew joined us a few minutes later. After breakfast, we left for the kaserne in Wuerzburg.

The M422 trainer projectile was in bad shape. It was dinged and dented all over, which was nothing we could fix. The markings were almost obliterated, though, so we began the maintenance procedure.

Wearing protective gloves and particle masks, we removed the nose cone from its base, revealing the black, depleted uranium rings inside. Depleted uranium emits alpha radiation, so we were protected by just wearing latex gloves and particle masks. Hooker and Thompkins removed the rings, one by one, and set them on a table. I began to clean them with a mixture of molybdenum and Freon, while Preston cut stencils with the machine and spray-painted the markings on the warhead: M422CA1E1.

In the event of a Soviet invasion of Germany, the invading army would hypothetically pass through the Fulda Gap to gain access to the

7. Nuke Training and Investigations

Rhine River. The Fulda Gap stretched from the state of Thuringia in the east to Hessen in the west, and if left unimpeded, enemy armor and infantry divisions could rapidly overrun Germany. NATO developed a strategy of nuclear deterrent, which included the weapons systems we were currently maintaining for artillery units, such as those assigned to the 3rd ID.

Defense of the Fulda Gap also included now-obsolete systems such as the Davy Crockett tactical nuclear recoilless gun and the SADM, which was a "backpack" nuclear device. Specialists were trained to parachute behind Soviet-occupied Europe with the SADM and use it to destroy enemy infrastructure. One of the older 55Gs I spoke with recalled working with the SADM for a short period of time before the program was scrapped in 1985.

Some of the artillery guys watched us. I noticed they had battle patches from the Gulf War, and one of them was a sergeant, though he couldn't have been older than 22.

"Blood stripes," mumbled Preston. He was upset because he was still an E-4 after five years in the Army. He had attended BNOC a year before, but still did not have enough promotion points for sergeant E-5. Peacetime made it hard for promotions, and being a 55G made it even harder. As nuke techs, we needed 950 promotions points to achieve E-5. This could take years because our field was small, and I could not see the Army having an MOS filled with nothing but NCOs and warrant officers.

At lunch, we secured our equipment and headed to the food court. I ordered some cheeseburgers and we all sat together to eat. Next to our table were some soldiers in Class As. They were wearing the red cord of the artillery on their right shoulders and had campaign badges from Iraq. We just sat there, no one saying a word. Sergeant Kilgens was the only one here who could relate to these men, since he was the only one who had been in actual combat. Seeing them made me feel inferior as a soldier, though I realized that what we were doing behind the scenes was very important to the overall mission of the VII Corps and European security.

The next couple of days became monotonous as we continued to clean and paint warheads and shipping containers. Thursday morning, we got to the kaserne at 8 and noticed that some artillery soldiers were in the room with the trainer projectile, laughing.

They had circled around a soldier, who was standing next to the training projectile. The bottom was opened, and I saw the DU (depleted uranium) rings on a table next to the projectile. They began egging the soldier on, calling out his name: "Adams! Adams! Adams!" The soldier grabbed one of the DU rings, stuck out his tongue, and proceeded to lick the whole surface of the ring around its circumference.

"What the hell is going on here?" shouted Sergeant Kilgens.

"Nothing sergeant," said one of the soldiers. "Just inducting a newbie into the platoon."

"Preston, grab the ANPDR/60," said Kilgens. "The rest of you stand there and don't move."

The artillery guys stood still. For sure the combat arms soldiers took rank more seriously than we did, as I saw previously at Baumholder. Preston returned with the radiac meter and Sergeant Kilgens put on a pair of gloves. He picked up a DU ring and held the face of the radiac meter to it. He set it at the lowest setting so it read only alpha radiation. The needle went haywire, bouncing back and forth. It produced the familiar static sound of a Geiger counter. The soldier who was being hazed looked at the readings, though I am sure he could not tell exactly what they meant. His face began to pale, and his eyes followed the needle as it bounced erratically. Kilgens turned the machine off and removed his gloves.

"Congratulations! You just gave your battle buddy cancer! Now get out of here!"

The soldiers scrambled out without a word. Kilgens turned to look at me.

"Is he really going to get cancer?" I asked.

"Probably not. He would need longtime exposure to become a cancer candidate. But maybe they'll think twice about acting so damn stupid."

We finished the day and headed back to the gasthaus for dinner. We were jubilant, and I decided to stay in for the night, since my urge to explore the city had vanished. After showering, I watched German TV, and there was a knock at the door. Thinking it was Hooker, I took my time getting there, until there was another firm knock. I realized that it was not Hooker and that it must be Chief Boyd or Sergeant Kilgens.

I opened the door, and to my surprise, two men were standing there, dressed in suits.

7. Nuke Training and Investigations

"Are you Private First Class Woodward?" the one in the gray suit asked.

"I am," I responded hesitantly. I didn't know what else to say, so I invited them in. I sat on the edge of the bed, while the gray suit sat down in the only chair in the room and the other man stood at the door.

"What's this about?" I asked.

"I am Agent Gorr, and this is Agent Dugan. We are with CID [Criminal Investigative Division]." I began to freak out. "We need to ask you some questions."

I nodded, not knowing what to say and completely in the dark. I had no idea why these men were in my room. I haven't done anything illegal; I haven't spilled government secrets, either legit or perceived, and I haven't stolen anything or killed anyone. I am only guilty of being utterly confused at their presence.

"We want you to know first that you are not in trouble." I felt a weight lift from my chest. "We are investigating a minor breach of security and need your help." Now my interest was piqued.

"Do you know a Specialist Kaminsky?" I nodded the affirmative. Then a barrage of questions started.

"How long have you known him? Have you ever seen him with classified material? Has he ever spoken with you about selling secrets? Who does he hang around with? Friends names? How long has he owned his car?" The questions kept coming. I answered what I could, and said, "I don't know" to the rest. My "I don't know" answers became so frequent that the agent snapped at me.

"I am sick of 'I don't know.' What can you tell me?"

Having grown up in the Chicago area, I learned early in life to keep my mouth shut when questioned. I helped many friends stay out of trouble with the police by dodging questions and sticking to "I don't know." Truth was, this time, I had no idea where they were heading with the questions.

The agent continued: "Do you know a German National named Georg?" I could not deny this fact, as they probably already knew the answer.

"Yes, I know him." The agent's face lit up, like he just discovered a new fact to whatever case they were working on. What the hell does Georg have to do with a CID investigation?

Last of the Glow Worms

"When was the last time you saw him?"

"Thanksgiving. We had a dinner at his place. Turkey, sweet potatoes, the whole nine yards."

"Was there any talk about what goes on at the depot or otherwise classified information?"

"Not that I am aware of, sir." The rest of the questions were mundane, just where I was from, how long I had been in the military, and other minor questions to gather as much information as possible. Agent Gorr reassured me that I was not in any trouble and stood up to leave. He handed me his card and nodded at Agent Dugan to open the door.

"Thank you for your time, Mr. Woodward. If we have any further questions, we will contact you."

"Have a good night," I lied, closing the door. I was restless the rest of the night and had a hard time falling asleep.

In the morning we packed up our equipment and headed back to Fischbach. The others started asking me questions about what went on with the CID and I told them everything that happened. I asked if anyone had heard anything about Kaminsky, but no one knew anything.

When we arrived back in Fischbach, I turned in all of my receipts and headed straight to Kaminsky's room to find out what the hell was going on.

He must have been expecting me, because he had beer ready after he opened his barracks room door.

"What the hell, dude? What did you do?"

He poured as he explained. He was using his car to drive to the admin bay in Area Two and picked up a confidential manual, which he was going to take to their workplace. He forgot about the manual being in the car, and he also forgot that he was selling his car to a German that evening. He sold the car, and later the German found the manual and, being a good citizen, turned it in to the MP station. Kaminsky's forgetfulness opened up a can of worms. I knew it was an innocent mistake, but I wanted to know how my name got involved.

"I gave your name as a character reference," he said, sipping a beer.

"And how the hell did Georg become involved?" He shook his head, either not knowing how or not wanting to say why. Though I was fuming, after a few beers, and his insistent begging for forgiveness, I dropped the whole subject.

I got the urge to travel again and called my cousin in France. She

7. Nuke Training and Investigations

told me things were still not cool there and that she was going back to Canada soon. I ended the conversation by promising to visit her there once I get out of the military.

I had been sending money back home every month for my parents to put into my savings account, which I kept open after I enlisted in the military, and I was left with just barely enough to survive. To save money on haircuts, I let my hair grow long, until Sergeant Kilgens yelled at me to get to the barber. I told him that I was broke, and he pulled a five-dollar bill from his wallet and forced me to go get the haircut. This happened at least once a month, much to my amusement.

By far Sergeant Kilgens was my favorite NCO. I teased him a lot, but I didn't say anything nasty or off color to him. He invited me to dinner at least once a month and I spent time with him and his wife. She was also from the South and had the same Southern drawl as my father's side of the family. I felt at home when I was with them, and the company gave me a reprieve from the homesickness I constantly felt.

Not long after the incident with CID, we had a barbeque at a lake in Ludwigswinkel. It was a popular spot for Americans to hang out in the summer, and the smell of barbequed ribs and hamburgers attracted Germans curious to sample American cuisine.

I was sitting with Hooker and Sergeant Kilgens when some girls approached us. They were not Germans; I could tell by their features that they were Slavic. I knew Hooker couldn't differentiate between European ethnicities, so I lead the conversation.

"Kako ste?" I said in Croatian. *How are you?*

"Oh," said the lead girl. She had a dark complexion, black hair and a pug nose. In broken English she said, "I thought you are Americans?"

"We are," responded Hooker, brushing me aside. I could not let Hooker get the best of me, so I switched to German.

"You are not Germans, right? Where are you all from?"

"Bosnia," the girl replied. "We just moved here." Her German was flawed, and I could detect the accent, just as she could probably detect mine.

"Govorite li Hrvatski?" she asked, switching to Croatian. *Do you speak Croatian?*

"Ne puno," I responded. *Not much.*

Hooker and Sergeant Kilgens were sitting there, listening to our strange conversation.

Last of the Glow Worms

"Ladies, please sit down," said Kilgens, interrupting the conversation. "Ever have American-style barbeque ribs?"

Satisfied after eating a plate of ribs and American potato salad, the girls opened up about their lives, switching to German for me to translate when they didn't know the words in English. Sergeant Kilgens pulled out an "A-game" that I had never seen before. He had them hanging on his every word; they were like schoolgirls with a crush on their middle-aged teacher. He told them stories from Vietnam and about the hundreds of places he's been to. He even pulled up his shirt to show them the scar that an vertical from his navel to the center of his chest, received during Vietnam from a mortar attack. I watched them as they leaned in closer to him, and I shook my head in disbelief.

Before they got up to leave, they gave Hooker a phone number to call them. The girls walked away with leftovers that Sergeant Kilgens gave them to take to their family. I sat there amazed at Kilgens' "game."

Taking a swig of beer, the sergeant leaned in close. "You see that?" He whispered, a smile growing from ear to ear. "That's how it's done, junior."

It was May of 1991, and we were called to a formation with the company commander. She briefed us on a training event that would be happening at the end of the week. It would involve a scenario in which the depot was being overrun by enemy forces. Area One will need to be secure or weapons stored there will need to be destroyed.

This was the first time that I heard an officer acknowledge what some of the other soldiers who did not work at the site had suspected.

We were told the training exercise would last until finished, which very well could be late into the night. The 165th would be involved, as it provides security, but the 41st Ordnance Detachment would not be present.

I felt excited about being involved in a training event of this magnitude. I got my gear ready and headed to the site with the M&A platoon. We hung out in the break room and Chief Boyd entered to brief us on our role in the event.

As the scenario went, the depot was being overrun. The MPs were fighting off the attackers with help from HQ platoon. We would be setting off the explosives to destroy the weapons; Alpha and Bravo platoons would be with us, providing transport and helping with the overall

7. Nuke Training and Investigations

execution of the mission. We would be assigned a partner and bunkers to wire for destruction.

We were split into three teams, which included the M&A, Alpha and Bravo platoons. I was with Specialist Thompkins, Specialist Hooker, Sergeant Kilgens, and some soldiers from the Alpha platoon. The rest of the nuke techs and Alpha and Bravo platoons are split into the other two teams.

We were on edge, but tried to make light of our anxiety by smoking and joking in the break room. We were in full battle gear, but we were not required to carry our NBC suits and gas masks. It was early evening, and the air was cool, which made wearing our gear more tolerable.

The MPs had stationed themselves in the watchtowers and in concrete fortifications that were scattered around the site. Humvees with M60 turrets drove slowly around the inside perimeter. I stood at the door of the M&A building and was awestruck at the sight of the security forces setting up positions. The MPs of the 165th were very professional and taking the training event seriously. There were no walkers among them; they hustled from place to place or to their positions in full battle gear. Watching them gave me the feeling that this was *real*, which was the effect the command was looking for.

Suddenly the signal sounded.

We rushed out of the M&A building with our guards. We heard "pop-pop-pop" all around us as the MPs engaged a group of soldiers playing the enemy. The blanks were going off all around us and we ran to our first bunker.

I had about a dozen keys swinging from my neck and I struggled to find the correct one to open the bunker's steel door. I got the key in its slot and waited until Thompkins got his key inserted. The air locks hissed and I jacked up the left door as Thompkins swung it out.

We rushed inside and began placing shape charges on top of the nuclear weapons containers. The trainer charges were hollow, and I stuck the detonation cord in place. We did this for the remaining 19 containers and rushed out of the building, unwinding the det cord as we rushed to the next bunker. We repeated the process, moving to the bunkers that were assigned to us. We met the next team as it left its last bunker and tied our det cords together. The team we met up with had already done this with the first team, so there was one continuous loop of det cord connecting all of the bunkers.

Area One view from the south, 1993 (courtesy Bernd Schwarz).

Sergeant Kilgens attached a final spool of det cord to the line and lead it to the M&A building. We got inside and waited for word on the outcome of the attack. Weapons were still firing outside of the secure area, though the familiar "pops" of blanks were dying down. It was late, around 12:00 a.m., when we received word the event was over and a success. The enemy was fought off and casualties were minimal.

We had a formation the next morning with the 165th MP Company present. The commander praised everyone on their performance and told us that she was proud of the soldiers stationed at the Fischbach Army Depot. There was applause once she finished speaking, and we were dismissed.

We celebrated that evening at the EM club. The atmosphere was jubilant until we discovered that a couple of soldiers are being discharged for getting DUIs.

I had heard about this and knew the two soldiers from the club. Two separate incidents had taken place, but the results were the same. Both were drinking and driving, and both crashed their cars. The German *polizei* picked them up and took them to the MP station in Pirmasens.

7. Nuke Training and Investigations

After an investigation, they were issued Article 15s and discharged under general conditions.

I realized that I had become fond of drinking too, maybe a little too fond. There was nothing around us, and if a person did not have a car, he was stuck on depot. The only pastimes we had were the bowling alley across the street or drinking beer. I started to believe that I needed to slow down, and this was reaffirmed by Chief Boyd one morning when I came to the site with bloodshot eyes after partying all night long.

Taking me aside, Chief Boyd began to give me the business about being top dogs on the depot, that we needed to act that way. He also did not like some of the guys that I hung around with at the club or off base (which included the two that were recently discharged). I was told to avoid them and to keep a straight path. I listened to what he said and promised him that I would focus on the future.

We went TDY at the end of May, this time to an artillery unit in Wertheim.

Wertheim was a small, medieval town located in the state of Baden-Wuerttemberg in southwestern Germany. It was quaint and a large red and white tower greeted us when we arrived. There was a large American military presence in the area, and, like Wuerzburg, Wertheim was populated with combat arms soldiers. Wertheim was home to the 72nd Field Artillery, one battalion of which was a nuclear artillery unit.

We performed the same tasks as in Wuerzburg, patching containers and remarking projectiles. Unlike Wuerzburg, though, I talked the others, including Chief Boys, into going out after work.

Not being familiar with the area, we wandered around aimlessly, and tired of walking, we headed into the nearest bar. We sat at the counter and ordered drinks before Thompkins and Hooker left to play pool on the other side of the room. I was sitting there with Chief Boyd, and we chatted about Army life and our hometowns. I found out he was stationed in South Korea, which he quickly discovered was a mistake, as I bombarded him with questions about life there. I wanted to go to South Korea and was thinking about re-enlisting just so I could go there. The only hold-up was promotion points; we needed 700 at a minimum to get stationed there, and I was nowhere near that goal.

The talk I had with the chief mellowed me out and I told him I was ready to leave. We told Hooker and Thompkins we were leaving, and they waved us away because there were some girls with them at the moment.

When we got back to the gasthaus, I said goodnight to the chief and retired for the night. I didn't have any nightmares and I woke up feeling well rested. We drove back to Fischbach and after unpacking realized that there were a few unfamiliar faces present.

One was a CW2, who greeted me, "Chief Vega. A pleasure." I took his hand and looked at Chief Boyd quizzically.

"Vega," said Chief Boyd, taking his hand. "I haven't seen you since Korea."

"And these two are Specialist Ruiz and Specialist Grogan. They PCS'd here from Fort Carson." I shook both their hands, and Chief Vega asked me to show Grogan around the depot. Ruiz would be living off base with her husband, but would also stay in the barracks until he arrived. I finished putting our equipment away and took them both to the barracks.

Ruiz was given a single room for herself on the first floor, while Grogan moved in with us on the second floor.

I took them both around the depot, giving the grand tour. We hit the EM club, PX, barber shop, library and dry cleaner, and we walked around to the old theater, then up the hill to the gym, finally winding our way back down to the barracks. The entire tour took 15 minutes.

I could tell by their expressions they were not entirely impressed with the depot, and I could only speculate that coming from a large base like Fort Carson to an isolated depot like Fischbach was a disappointment.

A cross raising ceremony across the border in France was scheduled for the next weekend. Hooker and Merkins asked me to go, but I declined. When they asked Grogan, he readily accepted.

Every year, a cross ceremony on a small hill in France commemorated World War II and the peace that followed. German, American and French people attended the ceremony and a celebration took place right after.

I had plans with Georg and did not want to ditch him to attend the ceremony.

Georg picked me up at the depot early Saturday morning. He was excited and said he had something to show me. We drove to his house in Reichenbach, and he took me into his basement.

7. Nuke Training and Investigations

It was dark and musty, but I saw two large shadows swinging above a table. A light clicked on and I was startled to see two wild boars.

"I got them yesterday," Georg said proudly. "*Wildschwein* is good to eat." He picked up two large carving knives. He began to saw through flesh and tissue, and I helped him as best I could. Coming from an urban area, I had no clue on how to clean an animal. Georg cut here, sliced there, and, in a few hours, there were chops, ribs, and bacon stacked onto plates.

That evening, we roasted the boar over an outside fire. His brother and sister and a few of his German friends were present. One of them I recognized; I had a small fist fight with him at one of the Rolling Disco Shows a few months ago. Neither of us got the better of the other, so the fight ended in a shouting match. When he recognized me, he smiled and handed me a beer. That put the situation to rest.

I stayed the night at Georg's house, and midday Sunday he drove me back to the depot. I took him to the PX to buy him a bottle of tequila as a thank you for the dinner. I knew he liked the stuff, and it was hard to get in Germany.

That night, I stayed in my barracks room and watched *The Silence of the Lambs*. I tried to identify with Hannibal Lecter, intelligent, methodical, detail-oriented, and a bit crazy, but I found myself more like Jodie Foster's FBI character, young, naive, and still hoping to find the best in people.

I was still 19 years old and saw myself as just having a good time. The Soviets still had a huge nuclear arsenal, and the situation there was volatile. The RAF had not attacked any U.S. installations lately, but this did not mean they were inactive. Then there was the Gulf War and the possibility of terrorist threats aimed at American soldiers in Europe.

I thought all the people and organizations that disliked America and would like nothing more than to cause chaos. American soldiers in Europe were potential walking targets, and I saw myself trying to have a good time in the midst of all that was happening in the world at the time.

8

Broken Arrow and the NWTI

One of the perks of being involved in the nuclear weapons program was the access to training that was not available to every soldier, only those with specialty MOSs. One such training was the Nuclear Accident/Incident Response and Assistance (NAIRA) exercise. NAIRA was a one-day training event that revolved around a hypothetical nuclear accident, which may or may not have resulted in an a nuclear detonation, but where radiation may have been released, and our duties as a response team to the detonation area. In the summer of 1991, we were briefed on the upcoming exercise and told we would be leaving the following Monday.

NAIRA was developed as a response to a "Broken Arrow" incident, the military's code name for an "unexpected event" involving a nuclear weapon. These events could include detonation, launching, firing, or the theft or loss of a weapon.

There had been a few previous Broken Arrow events in the U.S. military.

On January 24, 1961, a B-52 suffered damage on its right wing resulting in the release of two nuclear weapons. One weapon safely landed without breaking apart and was recovered. The second weapon broke apart near the town of Goldsboro, North Carolina. Some of the uranium was not recovered, but the area was claimed to be free of radiological contamination.

A B-52 collided with a KC-135 during a refueling mission near Palomares, Spain, on January 17, 1966. The B-52 was carrying four nuclear warheads; one weapon was recovered safely on land and another one at sea; the other two weapons hit the ground, resulting in the detonation of their high explosives and the release of radioactive materials. More than 1,400 tons of soil were removed to a safe location for storage.

8. Broken Arrow and the NWTI

To be involved in something as important as this exercise was why I joined the military. If I couldn't be deployed to a combat station, then there was nothing that I would rather be doing than working with nukes.

On the Friday afternoon formation before the NAIRA exercise, I was called to come to the front of the formation. I ran up there and stood at attention in front of the company commander. She read my promotion letter and pinned the Specialist E-4 rank on my collar. I heard applause and hoots and hollers, and the commander said, "Congratulations, Specialist Woodward." I returned to formation and was happy to finally be out of the "private" ranks.

We began to pack our equipment on the Sunday before the training began. In addition to our basic soldier gear, we also packed our NBC suits, gas masks, radiac equipment from the site, including ANPDR/60 Geiger counters and handheld dosimeters. Early the next morning, we left for the training area with a convoy of M35 "deuce-and-a-halfs," a couple of HUMVEES, a Chevy Blazer (painted camouflage green) and two Volkswagen minibuses (painted olive-drab). The MPs from the 165th Military Police Company, the 55Bs and some mess staff rode in the M35s with their equipment, and our platoon was split between the Blazer and VW minibuses.

We drove to a site about 60 miles from Fischbach, an open grass field about two square miles long. There were no signs telling me where I was, so I assumed that we were on another Army installation, though I did not see any gates that we passed through to suggest such. We parked our vehicles and began setting up our tents for the night. The mess staff began to prepare food, and after we were set up, we ate lunch. I never liked the meals in the field, and I ate grudgingly. The meals always seemed to be the same: roast beef, rice, French fries and cherry-flavored juice. The containers filled with water were always marked "potable," and sometimes the mess staff would fill them with unsweetened orange-flavored juice. I didn't know if they did that as a joke or on purpose to get people angry.

We finished our meals and were called to a formation. The personnel in charge of training had arrived and consisted of officers and NCOs. They began to explain the importance of the NAIRA exercise and everyone's role within it.

In the event of an accidental nuclear detonation, the Army's response would consist of four phases: notification, response, management and site recovery. The emergency response forces were divided into two groups: the IRF (initial response force) and the RTF (response task force). We were going to be training as the IRF, which included the MPs, nuke techs, ammunition specialists, and some medical staff who came to participate from a different unit. We were the first responders to a nuclear accident/incident and had to secure and monitor the area before the RTF arrived. After the briefing, we left formation and returned to our respective areas to prepare.

We sat around, waiting for the signal that started the event. We were not allowed to have alcohol on the training site, so we told tall tales about our lives back in the world. The warrant officers chuckled at my story about trying to find the lost treasure of Al Capone in the sewers of Lyons, Illinois (which just happened to be true). A few minutes into my story, an alarm sounded. We jumped up and started putting on our NBC gear. After putting on the chemical boots, I pulled my gas mask over my head and sealed it with a quick inhale while covering the side filters. I grabbed the radiac meter and rushed outside of the tent.

About 25 meters away, a shiny, round object was lying on the ground depicting the accident site. The story was an armed nuclear device accidently fell from transport, with the conventional explosives detonating, while potentially releasing radiation into the atmosphere. My platoon took our positions, forming a circle around the object, and we slowly began to approach it while reading radiation levels with the radiac meters. The trainers told us we were reading around 20 REMs (roentgen equivalent man), which was a minimal amount of released radiation from the weapon. The MPs began to set up a perimeter 50 meters from the accident site, with a guarded entry-exit to allow access to or departure from the accident site. There were a few soldiers playing casualties, and after taking initial radiation readings of area, we approached the casualties, ran the probe of the radiac meter over their bodies, and administered initial first aid if needed.

The accident victim I approached with Grogan had a broken leg and was bleeding from a laceration on his forearm. I pulled a wound bandage from my side pack and applied pressure to the laceration. Grogan wrapped gauze around my bandage, then called for a stretcher. Sims and Preston ran to us, and we put the casualty on the stretcher. They in turn ran the casualty to the makeshift hospital at the perimeter.

8. Broken Arrow and the NWTI

After the wounded soldiers were removed, EOD (explosive ordnance disposal) was sent in to inspect the weapon. We moved to a safe distance at the perimeter area and passed through the checkpoint. The EOD team began inspecting the weapon as we used our dosimeters to read the airborne radiation level at 100 meters. We were told the radiation levels were in an acceptable range and to proceed to the processing station to monitor the personnel entering and leaving the control area. I stood at the exit and had exiting soldiers stop and raise their arms to shoulder level. I ran the radiac meter over their arms, torso and legs. They were then told to remove their NBC gear and to put it in a small yellow container marked "waste" with the hazard symbol on the lid. We did this for every person leaving the area, until the last of the EOD personnel exited, and the all clear was signaled.

The training complete, we removed our gear and were called to a formation for debriefing. The trainers explained their observations on the techniques we used, where we did well, and where we needed improvement. After the debriefing, we were released from the formation to our tents. Grogan and I began packing up our equipment, while the others took the equipment to the vehicles. We then took the tent down, loaded it in the van, and hit the road back to Fischbach.

The next day, during our lunch hour, I rode with Merkins to the mess hall to get something to eat. Getting tired of eating ham and cheese sandwiches in my barracks room, I joined him at the mess hall.

Standing in the chow line, I stopped in front of the regular, everyday food that was offered. One of the mess staff, who I got along with pretty well, was standing in front of the food, handing out plates of sliced turkey, hamburgers or hot dogs. I smiled at him as I got there and asked for the sliced turkey. He shook his head no.

"You don't want that. Eat a cheeseburger," he said. Confused, I took him up on the offer and took two cheeseburgers. He smiled at me and I sat down in a booth. I never asked him why he pointed me to something different, and I didn't care to know the answer.

The mess hall was full today, and as I conversed with Merkins, I noticed unfamiliar faces. At first I thought that another training exercise was being performed by the German army here in Fischbach, but as the soldiers passed by, I realized they were Americans. I scanned the faces, not recognizing anyone. They must have been from a different ordnance company in Germany for some sort of training.

We got up to leave, and I took my tray to the trash bin. I scanned the faces again and a wave of familiarity washed over me. A girl I was with at Redstone Arsenal was among the faces. She was in my AIT class, a rather quiet girl with short brown hair, a clear complexion and piercing blue eyes. She was talking with the soldiers around her as they ate, and her gaze lifted and rested on me for a brief moment. I gave a shy wave, but she just looked at me as if I was a stranger, then returned to talking to the guys at her table. I couldn't tell if she didn't recognize me or just didn't care that I was standing in front her. I spent the rest of the day thinking about the incident and decided to try and find her after work. By the time we got back to the barracks, they were long gone.

Chief Vega informed us that we would be participating in the nuclear weapons technical inspection in February 1991 along with other nuke sites across Europe. During the inspection, the weapons systems were displayed and a briefing about the system was given by a member of our platoon to the visiting general. I was chosen by our crew chief to give the briefing for the M454 nuclear projectile. Chief Vega knew I had a fear of speaking in front of an audience, and he grinned as he handed me what I had to memorize for the visiting general. I had one week to prepare, and instead of training or calibrating equipment, I was standing in front of members of the platoon, reading my script. Naturally, they laughed and jeered at me, which only caused more grief and nervousness. The chief would calm me down and tell the others to be quiet. I would then repeat the script, over and over again, until I had it memorized. The chief was very supportive of my growing confidence.

"Don't worry about anything, Woody. If you screw up, it's only a three-star general and us who will know. You do know they report everything to VII Corps Commander General Spiglemire? You could become famous!"

I felt my face flush, and the chief walked away. Tomorrow was the inspection, and I went back to my barracks room and ignored the urge to drink some beer to calm me down. This was one of the rare evenings during my time at Fischbach that I did not drink. I didn't want to go in tomorrow red-eyed and blowing booze breath on a three-star general.

In the morning, I pressed my uniform and shined my jungle boots until they shone like mirrors. I chose my jungle boots because I hated

8. Broken Arrow and the NWTI

my basic training boots and I didn't own a pair of jump boots. I left my room and ran into Grogan, who was heading to the mess hall for breakfast. He was giving the briefing on the Pershing II and was confident in his speaking ability; he tried to make me even more nervous about mine. As we ate (omelets and toast), Grogan told me about a German girl he met the week before at a disco, making obnoxious sounds as he tried to imitate her actions in his barracks room. I began to lighten up and tried to push my nervousness to the back of my brain. We finished our meal and jumped in the waiting VW minibus with the rest of our crew. We laughed and joked on the way to the site. Grogan pointed to the mountains on the French side of the kaserne, noting that Celtic tribes used to live there and the Romans marched through 2,000 years ago on their Gallic conquest. We arrived at Area One and went through security. I noticed the MPs were also on edge; they would be performing an alert exercise for the visiting general. The daily routine with the MPs now involved a full vehicle search and two "numbers of the day." Luckily, I was not chosen, and I waited in the minibus as Grogan and Carter were frisked thoroughly. When they returned, we drove to the front of the M&A building.

I greeted the company commander when we entered, surprised to see her there. We walked into our maintenance bay and carted an M454 and M422 to the center bay. The missile crew wheeled in their Lance and Pershing II systems. I bent over the M454 and stood the shell straight up in its container, locking it in place. The PAL system on the nose cone consisted of a plastic combination lock, which was left on and in the locked position. I gave the projectile a final look. It was painted olive-drab with the lettering "M454" stenciled in black on its side. The container was pristine, similarly painted olive-drab and black stenciling marking the contents, without a single gouge or scratch on the surface.

I returned to the break room, where soldiers were sitting around, drinking coffee and smoking cigarettes. The chiefs, having been through an inspection before, once again told us to relax, everything would be fine. The company commander was also high spirited and in the middle of a Vietnam story when we were called to attention. An NCO entered the building, followed by a few lieutenants. This was the general's staff. They cleared an area in front of the door and the general walked into the room. I should say, he *glided* into the room.

I had never been this close to person of such high rank, and he oozed confidence. He greeted the room, telling us to be at ease. I relaxed and was then motioned by my chief to head toward my weapon system. Merkins was first with the M422 projectile, I was next with the M454 projectile, Grogan was third with the Pershing II missile, and Ruiz ended the lineup with the Lance missile. We stood at ease in front of our systems, waiting for the general, his staff and our chiefs to enter. I held my hands tightly at the small of my back; they were clammy from nerves. I did everything I could to keep my legs from shaking, even looking down at Ruiz, the only female presenter today. She stood calmly, then turned her head to look at me. She smiled and mouthed the words, "Don't worry." I wished I had her confidence and cursed myself as weak for being so nervous.

It seemed like hours before the general finally entered. He took his place five feet in front of Merkins, who began his presentation: "Sir, this is the M422 nuclear projectile, commonly known as the old 8-inch..."

I tuned out as Merkins made his presentation, focusing on my own panic. My left leg began to shake, and I pressed my foot down as hard as possible onto the floor.

"That concludes my presentation. Specialist Woodward will now continue with the briefing."

Okay, show time. The general walked to my station and stood directly across from me. His staff and our chiefs stood behind him. He smiled at me and I took that as the signal to begin.

"Sir, this is the M454 nuclear projectile, also known as the 1-5-5. It is an artillery-fired air-burst nuclear projectile which can be fired from the M114 and M198 howitzers. The M454 consists of the W48 or the W82 warhead. The W48 and W82 are similar in size and shape, but different in nuclear yield..."

While I was speaking, I saw movement behind the general. My crew chief, CW2 Rockton, was running his tongue around his lips and blowing kisses at me. I would have burst out in laughter if I hadn't been so focused on my presentation.

"Sir, we at the 64th Ordnance Company are currently supporting 7th Corps with this system. Specialist Grogan will now continue with the briefing."

"Good job, son," said the general. I was taken aback, since I had not heard him speak since his entrance.

"Thank you, sir," I replied, standing at attention. I watched as he reached into his pocket, pulled out an object, and gave it to me. It was a challenge coin for the 59th Ordnance Brigade.

"Thank you, sir," I said again. He nodded and walked to Grogan's system. Chief Rockton gave me a thumbs up as he walked away. I reached stealthily into my pocket and gripped the coin. This was one of the proudest moments of my military career.

The INF Treaty was signed by U.S. president Ronald Reagan and Soviet leader Mikhail Gorbachev on December 8, 1987, requiring the destruction of all tactical nuclear and conventional weapons with ranges between 500 km and 5,500 km. The treaty was in response to the nuclear arms buildup of the 1980s, which caused widespread protests throughout Europe and the United States.

The United States began a rapid buildup of intermediate-range nuclear missiles (Lance and Pershing II) in response to Soviet deployment of the new SS-20 Saber intermediate-range nuclear missile. The Saber had a range of more than 5,500 kilometers and could be launched from deep within Soviet territory. It was seen as a potential *offensive* weapon, in contrast to the Soviet SS-4 and SS-5 missiles, both of which had limited accuracy and were launched from immobile launchers which could be easily targeted by NATO missile systems. The range of the new SS-20 missile allowed for cities in western Europe to be main targets, including Bonn, Germany, and Brussels, Belgium. Western European leaders called for a response to the Saber deployment, which pressured the United States to deploy more tactical nuclear weapons throughout western and southern Europe. The escalating tension between the superpowers and the threat of MAD (mutually assured destruction) were both catalysts in bringing the Americans and Soviets to the bargaining table.

59th Ordnance Brigade Challenge Coin Awarded for Operation Silent Echo, 1992, Jeff Woodward (author).

I finally got a single room on the first floor of the barracks, toward the front entrance near the barracks phone. It was large, so I purchased a sofa and coffee table to put in front of the TV. My refrigerator was normal-sized, so I stocked it with beer, bread and lunch meat purchased from a local German deli in Fischbach.

The floor I kept clean and buffed, and to break the monotony of the beige cinder block walls, I hung a Yugoslavian flag near the door.

Later that evening, to celebrate, I filled a one-liter stein with beer and watched foam spill over the top. I put in *Silence of the Lambs*. To make the head of the beer go down quicker, I stuck my finger into the foam to accelerate the process. As I waited for the movie to start, there was a loud knock at the door. It was more like anxious pounding, and I yelled to whoever it is to come in.

To my surprise, Sergeant Kilgens opened the door with another NCO at his side. I had never seen this man before, and I looked at them in shock, an index finger in my beer.

"Woody, what the hell are you doing?!" barked Sergeant Kilgens. The NCO with him looked at me but didn't say a word.

"I'm making my foam go down, sergeant," I replied, still keeping my finger in the beer, and not standing up to greet them properly. Kilgens harrumphed and looked around the room, checking the cleanliness of it, I assumed, until his eyes rested on the Yugoslavian flag hanging on the wall. His face became like stone.

"Get that damn communist flag off of the wall!" he yelled. The other NCO stayed silent, but a grin formed on his face. This was a rare time that I actually saw Sergeant Kilgens legitimately angry. I knew the flag didn't mean anything; Yugoslavia was on the verge of breaking up, and I only bought it because I could not find a Croatian flag at the store.

I didn't want to upset Sergeant Kilgens any more than is, so I hesitantly pulled my finger from the beer and got up and removed the flag. He grinned at me in triumph and abruptly closed the door.

I had no idea why he showed up like he did, and the NCO at his side was a mysterious figure who came and went with no introduction. I looked at my beer stein and saw the foam had disappeared. I started the movie and fell back into the chair for a rare evening of solitude.

One morning in the spring of 1991 we were gathered together in the break room of the M&A building. Fifteen enlisted soldiers, myself

8. Broken Arrow and the NWTI

included, the platoon sergeant and two warrant officers were present. CW2 Vega began the meeting by telling us how important our mission was both to the 7th Corps and to the security of Europe.

Since the signing of the INF Treaty, both the United States and the Soviet Union had been preparing for the removal and eventual destruction of their tactical nuclear arsenals. For the Unites States, this would include all of the weapons systems present in Fischbach at the 64th Ordnance Company in addition to the other nuke sites in west Germany: the 27th Ordnance Company (Bueren), the 545th Ordnance Company (Muenster), the 619th Ordnance Company (Kriegsfeld), the 525th Ordnance Company (Siegelsbach) and the 9th Ordnance Company (Miesau). The casernes in Italy, Greece, Turkey and South Korea would also begin the process of disassembly and removal of nuclear warheads.

Our mission would involve disarmament and removal of the weapons systems, coordinating with the 165th MP for security. The weapons would be removed from Fischbach by helicopter, bringing the mission to an end. We would then begin TDY assignments to Ramstein AFB and Hahn AFB to make final inspections on the missile systems before they were shipped to CONUS (Continental United States).

Chief Vega paused, and I let what he said sink in. No nukes meant there was no mission for the 64th. No nukes also meant no mission for the 165th MP and the 41st Ordnance Detachment also stationed in Fischbach.

The primary mission of the 197th Ordnance Battalion and the 59th Ordnance Brigade as a whole *was* the storage and maintenance of nuclear weapons. Everything and everyone else revolved around that fact. Every medic, signal person, mess hall sergeant, supply clerk, MP, truck driver, ammo technician or mechanic from Pirmasens in southwestern West Germany to the Netherlands at the northernmost reaches was assigned to the 59th Ordnance Brigade to support the mission.

And now that mission was coming to an end.

Later that evening, while hanging out in the EM club with some other soldiers, drinking beer and listening to music, I decided not to bring up what was going to be happening at Area One. It was strange. They had an idea of what was stored in the area, but it never came up in conversation, and I never said anything about what we were doing within those eight-foot fences, topped with razor wire and surrounded by watchtowers. I knew their MOSs, I knew everything about them personally, as they did about me. I knew some were truck drivers and others were mechanics. But most did not ask questions about what happened on-site.

Since the upcoming weeks were going to be hectic, I decided to let my girlfriend know that I would not be around so often for a few months. She was a German national and also had no idea what my job was. Whenever she asked, I would just respond, "Toilet cleaner," and laugh it off. In any event, she was certain that Fischbach stored chemical weapons, just like every other German national within a 100-mile radius.

Until 1988, Greenpeace and other activist groups held protests outside of the entrance gate to the kaserne against the alleged storage of poison gas and nerve agents in the depot. This stemmed from an article in the *Stern* magazine from August 18, 1982, which stated that the Fischbach depot was home to upwards of 10,000 pounds of VX and GB nerve gas. The *Stern* has a readership of almost 1.6 million per week and reached many Germans who were concerned about nuclear or chemical weapons in their country. Say it was a "call to arms"—every year since the publication there have been annual protests in front of the gate. This had not happened since I had been stationed at Fischbach, but some of the other soldiers who were recalled that it was always a mess.

In 1988, the protesters lined up along the fence line of the depot, holding signs that read *"Giftgas: Mit uns Nicht!"* (Poison Gas: Not for Us!) or "Army Go Home!" among other things. The SOP would be for the MPs from the 165th to secure the gate and park Humvees and trucks in front of it. They would have one mounted gunner with an M60 and form along the fence line. At this particular protest, the demonstrators decided to stage a sit-in, disrupting traffic. The *polizei* showed up and arrested a few for "attempting to provoke arrest." After a few hours, the protesters left, but not before they put up decals on road signs and trees, letting everyone who drove past know that Fischbach was home to chemical weapons.

Though I was not present for the protests, I did hear often from German nationals about the chemical weapons stored in Fischbach.

I was out one evening at a small pub in Busenberg with a German friend of mine. We ordered a *weinschorle*, white wine mixed with mineral

8. Broken Arrow and the NWTI

water. At this particular pub, the weinschorle was served in a chalice, which held a liter of the drink. We sat at a table with some Germans my friend was acquainted with; I had never seen them before. We all took turns using a large silver ladle to drink from the chalice. As we became more relaxed from the alcohol, I noticed the others asking questions about where I was stationed. My German wasn't fluent, but I knew enough to hold a conversation, and I usually kept that fact to myself. When they learned I was stationed at Fischbach, they began to question my friend about the supposed chemical weapons stored there. I knew where they were going with the questioning, and I asked jokingly if they were RAF members. They laughed and said no, they were Greenpeace.

This was one of the moments during my time in Fischbach when I wanted to jump up and scream, "There are no chemical weapons in Fischbach, you dolts, only nukes!" It took everything I had to control myself. I was warm from the alcohol, and not feeling very confrontational. I ended up replying: "I don't know what they store there. I only clean toilets."

Hooker snagged me up for the weekend, and we took another trip to Brussels. The day was beautifully sunny, with the sunlight reflecting off the spires of churches and the stained glass of medieval buildings. We stopped at a cafe and sipped on espressos, watching a Belgian soldier across the cobblestone street guarding a building. His light beige uniform was neatly pressed and a rifle rested on his right shoulder. He marched 15 feet, stops, does an about face, and marches back to his starting position. There were no markings on the building, so we couldn't tell who or what he was guarding.

We spent the day visiting Gothic churches, whose architecture was amazing to see firsthand, shopping at small boutiques, and sampling different food at small shops run by Arabs. We finally settled into a cafe that was quite full of patrons and had no empty tables. Hooker wanted to leave, but I begged him to stay and have a beer. He told me he was going to leave and would be back in a little while to get me, then left without saying goodbye. I decided not to chase him and scanned the room until I spotted an empty chair at a table where an older man and woman were sitting.

I walked to the table and asked in English if I could sit down. The old man's eyes brightened and he said, "Of course" in a slightly French accent. I took a seat, and, without asking, the old man called a waitress over and ordered a beer for me.

"Thank you," I said gratefully. The old man was wearing a light brown overcoat, and the top of his eyeglasses covered his bushy gray eyebrows. He was thickset and his fingers reminded me of sausage links.

The woman he was with was thin, almost skeletal, and her clothes hung on her, including the shawl that was wrapped around her neck. She must have been in her mid-fifties, and even the most casual of glances said that she was a looker when she was younger. Her eyes were glassy from the alcohol, and when she forced a smile, I noticed a bottom tooth was missing.

We began chatting, and from the start I could sense that something was not right with the older couple; they seemed to be brooding over their drinks, putting on fake smiles as they conversed with me. One beer turned into many, and they became more open, talking about the state of affairs in Belgium, the United States and Russia. They were grateful the Americans had bases in western Europe to protect them from the communists, but also hopeful for the future of a united Germany and peace in Europe.

I was quite buzzed by now, but the old man kept buying me drinks. I didn't want to be impolite and refuse, but my stomach was starting to push back against the alcohol. The old man finally said something personal. "We lost our son a year ago, on this day, to cancer. He was 31 years old, and a most wonderful son, one that a father could be proud of." The old man's eyes filled with tears. "One year ago today," he repeated.

The woman now had tears forming in the corners of her eyes. I saw one tear slip down her face. Watching them in sadness almost brought me to tears.

"I am sorry for the loss of your son," I replied, not knowing how to properly respond. I clapped the man on the shoulder.

After finishing my last beer, I told them I had to leave. They tried to stop me, asking me to come back to their apartment for something to eat. I politely declined, saying I needed to find my friend. I waved at them as I walked out of the cafe, and they sadly waved back.

Stumbling around Brussels, I finally found the car. Hooker had still not been there, so I decided to rest in the back seat. It was still early evening, but drinking during the day made me tired.

8. Broken Arrow and the NWTI

I woke up, and it was dark outside. Still groggy, I looked in the front seat, and Hooker had still not arrived. Needing to find a bathroom, I left the car and started to walk down the street. Few people were about, and the sun was now beginning to rise, casting an orange glow on the building facades. I walked aimlessly, in vain trying to find a place that was open. Frustrated, I turned down an alleyway and kept walking until I saw a short flight of concrete steps, which looked like the back entrance to a restaurant. I took a seat on the top step and leaned against the railing. Sleep took me again, until I was woken by someone tapping me on the shoulder.

"Sorry," I said instinctively. The man standing behind me shook his head, leading me to believe he did not speak English. He waved for me to come into the opened back door of the restaurant. I followed, and he guided me to a stool at the bar. The place was dark, and tables in neat rows covered in white cloth were being set for the day by a busboy. The man behind the counter poured me a cup of coffee and went into the kitchen. I sipped on the coffee until he returned, carrying half a loaf of bread and a small dish of butter. "Thanks again," I said, and he just smiled. I sliced the bread, smeared it with butter, and began eating. The man continued working, cleaning cutlery and using a towel to wipe down wine glasses.

After finishing the bread, I put some German marks on the counter. He shook his head and smiled, pushing the money back to me. I once again thanked him and walked out of the restaurant to find Hooker.

The whole experience had me befuddled, until I realized that the man had been nice to me for one reason.

He thought I was homeless.

I found Hooker at the car, sitting in the driver's seat. "Let's go, bro!"

Too tired to argue, I let the car's rocking back and forth as we drove put me to sleep.

The operation would be starting the week of May 1, 1991, and we began by preparing our calibration and testing equipment. We had new NBC gear issued to us, the white, full-body suits like in the movies when scientists were dealing with aliens. We went over the operation on the trainer systems; since I was assigned to the projectile crew, we went over the LLC (limited life components) we would be removing from the warheads. There were manuals to be followed, with instructions for each step of the process. In the crew, we would have one person giving out tools, two disassembling the projectile, and the crew chief reading the instructions out loud from the manual.

The MPs would be providing security and would need to be present during the operation. They would be guarding the main entrance to the M&A building and have two guards posted inside of the maintenance bay as the weapons were transported in for disassembly and back out again after they were finished.

Members from Alpha and Bravo platoons would be assisting in loading the helicopters with the containers. Only the 55Gs were allowed to be in the bays until the components were removed and the weapons reassembled.

We were to move the weapons containers from the bunkers inside of the perimeter of Area One and into the M&A building under armed escort from the MPs. After completion, they were to be moved back into the bunkers. When the mission was completed, the weapons systems would be transported out of the depot by Chinook helicopters, which would be landing at the helipad inside of Area One. They would then be transported to Ramstein AFB, where they would eventually make their way back to the United States.

We trained for two weeks before the word came that the mission was starting. I was excited; I knew this moment was historic. I celebrated the night before mission launch by getting drunk at the EM club with the usual crew.

Suffering a small hangover the next morning, I jumped into the VW minibus with my fellow 55Gs, and drove to Area One. There was much commotion at the gate; MPs were scrambling to get prepared. The sun had just risen over the mountain to the east.

Operation *Silent Echo* had begun.

9

Operation *Silent Echo*

We began bright and early Monday morning, and the platoon gathered in the break room. Outside of myself, the two warrant officers, Boyd and Vega, were present; they would be guiding their respective crews through the mission. The rest of the platoon was present, waiting for the MPs to arrive so we could begin.

The break room was filled with cigarette smoke, and Chief Boyd was standing next to the coffee machine, pouring cup after cup, and gulping down the black liquid piping hot. Chief Vega began to tell us about Fort Lewis, Washington, and how beautiful the scenery was there at this time of year. Sergeant Kilgens began to taunt him, telling him how beautiful Vietnam was at this time of year. I found the bantering amusing.

The MPs started arriving at 9:00 a.m. They greeted everyone as they entered and sat down in the open chairs. They leaned their rifles against the chair arms and removed their helmets. I noticed that one was female, surprised because I had not seen her before. She stood about six feet tall and looked as if she could handle herself well in an emergency. These two would be our inside guards, coordinating with the MPs outside the building as to when the weapons were finished and needed to be returned to their bunkers.

Chief Boyd removed himself from the coffee machine and walked to the bay door.

"Let's go everyone." We stood up and headed to our bays. Our white NBC suits were rolled out, and we began to get dressed. I pulled mine over my BDUs, and the suit was very tight, making me look like a marshmallow. I watched Hooker slide his suit on, and he flexed at me once it was on. If cameras were allowed, this would have been the perfect shot. Paris, Belgium, Switzerland, and the bay inside a nuclear weapons site.

After our suits were on, we took turns duct taping our gloves to our forearms, as we had during the NAIRA exercise. Once we were fully protected, I was told to push one of the M454 containers into the containment room in the corner. To my amusement, I noticed the mushroom cloud I had drawn in grease pencil at the onset of the Gulf War was still on the Plexiglas. We removed the cover of the container and placed nylon cargo straps underneath the projectile. Hooker and Merkins lifted the projectile from the container and placed it onto a stand. They tightened the two metal clamps that wrapped around the body and Sergeant Kilgens turned the crank handle, which rotated the projectile to an upright position. The bottom of the projectile was supported by a plate which was welded onto the stand and Chief Boyd inspected the weapon to make sure it was secure. Nodding, he moved to the side of the room, picked up a manual stamped "Secret," and opened it to skim over the instructions. He told me to get the tools ready, small ratchet wrenches, needle-nose pliers, sockets with strange shapes, and other items. I lined the tools carefully on the table, which is covered in a white cloth.

Chief Boyd began to read the instructions. Two people were needed to remove the components, and they had to ground themselves to the weapon. I handed Hooker a spanner wrench, which he used to remove the nose cone. He handed me the nose cone, and I set it on the parts table. I then handed Hooker and Merkins a grounding strap with an alligator clip at each end. This was attached to a black strap, which would go around the tech's wrist. Merkins and Hooker put on the wrist straps and attached themselves to the projectile for a ground. Chief Boyd then slowly read the next set of instructions. Hooker's hands moved slowly as he took pieces out of the warhead and handed them to me. I set them carefully on the parts table and waited as they dug deeper into the warhead.

A few more pieces were removed before the component we needed to get at was exposed. Chief Boyd told me which specialty tool to get ready and I handed it to Hooker. He reached in the warhead, turned the ratchet a few times, and handed the tool back to me. With both hands he pulled out a stainless steel tube and handed it to me. I took it with both hands and set it in a Kevlar container made specifically for this component. I closed the container and handed a radiac meter to Sergeant Kilgens, who had been watching the procedure from the

9. *Operation* Silent Echo

corner. He turned the machine on and ran the probe over the warhead. He nodded as the readings were within normal range of an exposed device.

We began to reassemble the warhead and install the components in reverse order. I quickly handed and took tools back and forth to Hooker and Merkins, and with a final turn of the spanner wrench, the nose cone was back in place and secure.

Sergeant Kilgens cranked the handle until the warhead was horizontal. We removed the straps and carefully placed the weapon back into the container. I pushed the container to the wall and brought another to the work room. Chief Boyd called for a break before we began the next round.

The whole process, from bringing the container into the room, removing the component and pushing the container back out again, took just under two hours. As we were putting the test equipment away, I stumbled on a container and fell, holding the radiac meter out in front of me so it wouldn't hit the floor. I landed on my back and my elbows smacked hard into the concrete. Everyone rushed over to help me up. The radiac meter was saved from damage, to the detriment of my body.

I asked to go to the clinic the next morning, and Merkins drove me to Münchweiler. I sat in a chair in front of the check-in counter, along with other soldiers who were here for various reasons. Many came here to get a profile, and a "shaving" profile was one of the most common I had seen.

I waited my turn, tapping my boot on the floor impatiently. One by one the soldiers were called to examination rooms. Finally, my name was called.

The doctor began with a regular physical, checking my heart rate and lungs. He asked me why I was here.

"I fell and landed on my elbows," I told him.

"And how did that happen?" he asked. This was a moment when I decide to refrain from telling an officer what was going on in Fischbach. How could I explain that we were just taking LLC components out of a nuclear warhead when I tripped and fell over a nuke container?

"I tripped in my room. Fell over a chair," I lied. He examined me further and told me that all was well, nothing broken or sprained, and wrote me a prescription for Tylenol 2 to ease the pain.

Everyone on the depot was abuzz with what was happening at the site. Those that didn't work there asked questions, and those who were involved didn't say anything. The exception was the ammunition specialists, who were excited at being part of something as big as *Silent Echo* and were talking freely about what was happening. I found this out at the EM club, where I was asked about what was going on. I played dumb and told them we were moving containers around the site, that's all. Nothing else.

In the next few weeks, we started knocking out the disarmament of the warheads like a well-oiled machine. We took turns working on the warheads and rotated roles on every other projectile. At the end of the third week, we had the time down to under an hour per warhead. We were halfway through the projectiles, while the second crew was almost complete with the disarmament of the Pershing IIs and Lances. I did not get a chance to work with them, but I was told that when we got to Ramstein and Hahn AFBs, we would be working with the systems sent there for disarmament.

I sat in the break room with the rest of my crew, wearing my white NBC suit, while the missile crew continued working in its bay. Two MPs were sitting there also, joining in on the conversation about the beating of Rodney King that had taken place earlier in the year. As MPs, they naturally support the LAPD and started giving their reasons why the man deserved what he got. I viewed it differently and started giving my reasons why I thought the beating went overboard. Suddenly, one of the MPs snapped at me, telling me I didn't know what I was talking about, I was never a law enforcement officer, and I didn't know what they went through every day on the job, etc.

I really didn't want to get into an argument with him and started to say something off topic to deflect his anger when second crew came running toward the door from the bay. We jumped up as they ran in yelling. The female MP grabbed the steel entry door to the bay and slammed it shut, engaging the lock. She grabbed her rifle and raised it while the MP I was about to argue with also jumped up and got his rifle into position.

"What happened?" the female MP yelled. Her helmet tipped to the left, as if it were too big for her head. "What's going on?"

Chief Vega, who was the last person through the doorway, gave the MPs a sly grin. I got a flashback to last year when the same thing happened when Merkins supposedly saw a mouse.

9. *Operation* Silent Echo

The freaked-out MPs just stood there, unsure of what to do. The silence was deafening, and everyone was waiting for Chief Vega to speak.

Chief Vega cleared his throat, then said with a smile, "Just testing you."

On Friday night, I left for my girlfriend's apartment in Pirmasens to spend the weekend with her. I usually took the bus to Husterhoeh Kaserne in Pirmasens, then walked to her apartment across town. I passed the Parkbräu brewery, which had been making beer in this area since 1888. Its most popular beers were Pils and Export, sold in .333ml or .500ml bottles. It also produced a beer which was very popular among American soldiers called "Pirminator," which was 16 percent alcohol but was very smooth to drink.

I walked past the brewery and turned left onto Schlossstrasse. I passed small Turkish resale shops and an adult bookstore before passing the McDonald's on the corner in front of the Exezierplatz. I decided to stop at the music store, The Wave, on the way. It was popular among Americans because it sold heavy metal, punk and techno CDs, which were rarely available at the PX. It also allow you to listen to the CD before you purchased it and had listening stations with headphones set up for this purpose. I stayed there a little longer than I wanted and ended up buying a Dead Kennedys CD before leaving.

I continued walking and headed up the Blocksbergstrasse to the Berlinerringstrasse. My girlfriend's apartment building was on the corner of Eybergweg, and I stopped at the Avia gas station to pick up a bottle of cognac.

The apartment was filled with people, including her brother and his friends. We were cordial but did not hang out together, though we had the same tastes in music and movies. I waited in the living room, drinking a glass of cognac while my girlfriend got ready for our date.

It was 9:30 before we left, and almost ten before we hit the club, which was called the Roundup. The Roundup was frequented by Germans and American soldiers, most of whom were stationed in Pirmasens or Münchweiler. We sat at a table in the back and ordered drinks. I scanned the room, not recognizing anyone, German or American. Hanging out in Pirmasens was relatively new for me; in Fischbach we frequented the clubs and discos closer to the depot because trying to make it to the last bus out of Pirmasens was too risky.

We were drinking and having a good time, dancing to some songs, and sitting out others. The club was darkly lit, and a DJ played music from a small booth near the entrance. Vanilla Ice must have been the most requested artist this night, because he must play "Ice Ice Baby" three times an hour. I started to get homesick, not for Chicago, but for Fischbach.

Through the bottom of my glass, I saw a group of Americans gathering. They were forming a circle around one guy, who seemed to be upset, though I could not hear what he was saying over the music. One of the Americans started scanning the room, and to my dismay set his eyes on me. He tapped another guy on the shoulder, and they started walking toward our table. I felt my stomach tighten up. I had never been in a fight with another American, and I hadn't been messing around with anyone's girlfriend.

They approached the table, and stood there, looking down at me. The one who seemed agitated began to speak.

"Are you American?" he asks me, confident that I was.

In the past, I had played games with other Americans. For example, in the Wave music store, I was digging through used CDs when someone tapped me on the shoulder.

"Excuse me, do you speak English?" The person who wanted my attention looked at me as if I owed him an answer. He didn't ask me if I spoke English; it sounded more of a demand.

"Ne, ich spreche kein englisch," I responded, using my best German skills to sound authentic. He looked at me, thought about it for a moment, then walked away.

"Yes, I am American," I responded to the guy hanging over my table. My girlfriend got up to dance with some friends.

"How do you feel about racism?" he asked. I did not know where this question was coming from or where it was going. I didn't answer and just stared at him until he continued.

"One of our friends just got beaten up by skinheads." He pointed to the door. "They are right outside, and we're getting everyone together to go out there."

I was really in no mood to go out and fight with a bunch of drunken skinheads, but I told him I'll go. Maybe I felt obligated to help fellow American soldiers, even though I didn't know them. He shook my hand, and I got up to follow him. I walked to the dance floor first and told my girlfriend that I'd be right back and followed the crowd outside.

9. *Operation* Silent Echo

The street was dark, and there were a few people standing in front of the club. I followed the pack of soldiers up the street until we get to the corner. I looked to my left, then to my right. The street was empty. The crowd of Americans was confused by the absence of the skinheads, so they headed back to the club. Along the way, they started throwing their beer bottles at parked German cars. One of them, a stocky guy about 5'4", jumped up on the hood of car and began to jump up and down. Moments later, there were Americans yelling and screaming, throwing beer bottles and damaging cars. I walked to the front of the club and watched the scene. I heard the familiar whine of *Polizei* sirens and decided it was time to get back inside the club.

The *Polizei* did not play around when it came to damaging property, especially when American soldiers were the perpetrators. They did not carry guns but had rubber batons that they were fully authorized to use on disorderly Americans. There was no talking back to them; if a person began to smart off, he get a nice whack from the baton.

We hung around the club until 2:00 a.m., closing time. The club immediately lit up brightly when the fluorescent bulbs switched on. Cigarette smoke hung like a cloud above the dance floor, and the DJ abruptly stopped playing music. The only sounds left were glasses and bottles clinking together and drunken banter from the patrons, who began to shuffle toward the exit. It was a motley mix of Germans and Americans, and some stopped to chat outside on the sidewalk. I wondered about the scene; 50 years ago, a dreadful war was raging in Europe, the Americans and Germans were bitter enemies. Yet, decades later, both countries were stalwarts of the NATO alliance and formed the front line of the Cold War.

The weekend passed by quickly, and Monday morning found me back at Area One, playing with nuclear warheads. We were almost finished disarming more than half of the M454s, and the missile crew was completely finished with its mission disarming the Lance and Pershing II warheads.

Chief Vega told us that the first Chinooks would be here to transport the Pershings and Lances to Ramstein Air Force Base on Thursday. The missile crew would begin helping us with the projectiles to help finish the mission.

We split the projectiles between the two bays and worked in two

Last of the Glow Worms

teams. We ere averaging about an hour per warhead and had a few dozen left before the mission was complete.

In between working on warheads, we entertained each other in the break room by hacking on the MPs. Contrary to popular belief, the majority of 95Bs performed security detail in a variety of functions, instead of actually being law enforcement officers who pulled people over for speeding on base or investigating crimes committed by soldiers. Recently promoted Sergeant Preston was poking fun at the two MPs on security detail inside of the M&A building, asking them off the wall questions, such as "Where's your billy club?" "If someone breaks in, will you breathe on them with that nasty breath of yours to knock 'em out?" "I could have been an MP, but my GT score was too high." Preston was relentless, and I could see the male MP becoming agitated. The female guard took it in and even laughed at some of the more crude statements that Preston made. This went on for about 15 minutes, before the outside door swung open and a second lieutenant walked into the room. The male MP yelled, "Attention!" and everyone jumped up and stood, except for Sergeant Preston, who ignored the officer and walked to the coffee table for a cup of coffee.

I had seen this lieutenant on depot before, but he must have just arrived, because we didn't know his name, just his face. I didn't know if he is with the 165th MP Company or an officer assigned to Alpha or Bravo platoons, and I really didn't care who he was; he had just interrupted Sergeant Preston, who was in rare form just moments ago.

The officer said, "At ease," and we went back to what we were doing, which was waiting for Preston to begin with the MPs again.

The officer waited, as if expecting someone to address him. We all sat there silently until the female MP asked him if he needs anything.

"I will be assisting with the airlift on Thursday, coordinating with the pilots on arrival, loading, departure, and unloading of the 'specials.'" I silently snickered at the word "specials." This officer was truly new in Fischbach.

"How is the mission progressing? Will we be ready on Thursday morning?" The lieutenant was looking at Sergeant Preston, who was the ranking soldier in the room.

Assuming he was supposed to reply, Preston responded. "Yeah, we are almost ready. Just about a dozen more projectiles to go."

The officer looked at him, perturbed. He put on a hard face and

9. Operation Silent Echo

cleared his throat. "Sir," he said, meaning that Sergeant Preston should be calling him so. It took Sergeant Preston three seconds to turn, look at the female MP, and continue speaking.

"Once the projectiles are finished, they will be pushed back into the bunkers to wait for transport." The MP was confused, and the second lieutenant's face turned into a scowl. Preston kept talking to the MP about the mission, completely ignoring the officer. The lieutenant got the hint and stormed out of the building defeated. We laughed as soon as he exited, and Preston told us it was time to get back to work.

By Wednesday evening, the mission to disarm the complete nuclear arsenal at the 64th Ordnance Company, Fischbach Army Depot, was accomplished. Every M454, M422, Lance and Pershing II was rendered useless and ready for departure. We celebrated at the EM club, taking turns buying each other drinks. Everyone was present, even Vega and Boyd. I tried to make them drink shots, but they declined.

Warrant officers were the technical experts of their given MOS. They attended WOCS (Warrant Officer Candidate School) to become specialists in their fields.

The proper way to address a warrant officer was "Sir," "Chief" or "Mr." We usually just said "Chief" without using their last names while addressing them personally, very rarely calling them "Sir." When speaking about a certain warrant officer when he was not present, we said "Mr.," as in "Mr. Boyd," or "Chief," for example, "Chief Vega is on his way to the site." Their ranking system follows CW1 through CW5, which is the highest rank a warrant officer can obtain.

I had a deep respect for warrant officers, and I was interested in applying for WOCS after I made E-5. They were down to earth and not as pompous as some of the regular officers were. Commissioned officers treated the WOs with respect, knowing that their expertise was indispensable.

Early Thursday morning, we reported to Area One and waited in the M&A building as the MPs and soldiers from Alpha and Bravo platoons prepared for the air transport of the warheads.

We were not allowed to travel with the Chinooks and had been tasked with moving the containers outside of the bunkers, with Alpha and Bravo platoons loading them into the helicopters. They would be riding in the Chinooks with MP guards to unload at Ramstein, then fly back to Fischbach to take another load.

Last of the Glow Worms

The break room had become hustle and bustle as MPs, ammo specialists from Alpha and Bravo platoons, nuke techs and officers got prepared for the departure. The company commander and first sergeant were present, and Lieutenant Westmayer, the officer I performed staff duty with in the past who was platoon leader of Bravo platoon, was also present. He would also be flying to Ramstein and was dressed in his battle gear complete with rifle.

The building began to shake, signaling the arrival of the first helicopter. I stood outside the building to watch as it landed, a truly remarkable machine with two large propellers spinning so fast they give the illusion of rotating in slow motion.

Chinooks had been in military service since the mid–1960s and were used during the Vietnam War. The twin-engine, tandem rotors of the Chinook allowed for heavy lifting, and its primary role included troop transport and battlefield resupply. A staple of NATO, the Chinook was as recognizable to the West as the Soviet MIL-Mi24 attack helicopter was to the East.

I stood in awe as the helicopter begins its descent. There was one

Nuclear warhead storage bunkers at Area One, 1993 (courtesy Wiebke Trott).

9. Operation Silent Echo

helipad Fischbach, and the pilot began to slowly lower the helicopter onto it. The rotors caused a storm of wind to push against me, and dust and dirt started to batter the outside of the building. I covered my eyes and went back inside.

The pilots entered shortly after landing. They were dressed in olive-drab aviator uniforms. One of the pilots was a woman with short gray hair, wearing a colonel's eagle on her lapel. Sergeant Kilgens whispered to me that she was the first female pilot in the U.S. Army, Sally Murphy, and the only female helicopter pilot. I wished I had a camera with me; like a star-struck fan, I would have rushed her for an autograph and a photo opportunity.

The pilots took seats and were good humored. They would be waiting in the break room while the Chinook was loaded. The MPs were already outside, and the ammo specialists were ready for the move, standing in front of the bunker, fully geared. Our platoon headed to the first bunker to be emptied. The MPs in the main guard shack disabled the WADS system, and Merkins and I took turns inserting our keys into the lock box to deactivate the air locks. When the door swung open, the ammo specialists entered with us to move containers out of the bunker. We had a window; the Soviet satellite had passed, and they began pushing the containers into the Chinook's cargo hold.

I watched as the containers disappeared inside. One after another, they were rolled up the ramp and out of sight. The ammo specialists were very professional and working hard to get the first load airborne.

Once again, I stood outside as the first load left the depot. The wind pressed against me as the helicopter ascended, once again pushing dirt into the air. I learned a lesson from earlier and put on a pair of safety glasses to watch the helicopter as it departed. This was the first load of many to come. When the helicopter was out of sight, I looked at the Eye of Ludwigswinkel on the hill overlooking Area One. If the Germans did not know something was going on at the depot, they would soon.

I met with Georg on Saturday afternoon to go to the Teufelstisch, a sandstone rock formation in the neighboring town of Hauenstein. The "Devil's Table" is a large rock sitting atop a naturally-formed pedestal.

"So what's going on in Fischbach?" he asked me.

"They're just moving stuff around," I said. I couldn't deny that helicopters had been flying in and out of the depot; the move was too big to keep quiet.

"Poison gas?" he asked me with a stoic look on his face.

"Nah, Georg, not poison gas. I don't know what they're moving, but it's not poison gas, man."

"Ok." His simple response lightened the mood, which could have quickly gone the other way if he had kept pressing me. I suspected he knew I was lying to him, but he showed no indications of being angry.

"Let's go get some beer," he said happily.

With that, the subject was dropped.

Over the next couple of weeks, the helicopters continued airlifting the warheads out of the depot. We worked frantically, trying to complete the mission as quickly and safely as possible.

Hooker and Merkins were both ETSing at the end of one week and heading back to the States. I felt sad at their leaving; we bonded well, and I considered them brothers. Stationed on a depot as small as Fischbach, you either become close with those around you or you push them away. I had seen soldiers come and go, and I had only had a strong connection to a select few of them.

I knew Hooker would be going back to the East Coast, while Merkins returned to Georgia. Both planned to attend college, and judging by their personalities, I felt sure they would do well. We exchanged phone numbers and addresses, and I prayed that we would stay in touch.

Sergeant Kilgens and Chief Vega would be rotating stateside by the end of the month. I would be left with Chief Boyd, Specialist Grogan, Specialist Ruiz and Sergeant Preston. We ere the last 55Gs in Fischbach.

The 41st Ordnance Detachment removed the Pershing II and Lance missile sections from Fischbach by land transport while we were removing the warheads by helicopter. After their mission was completed, they began the move of the entire 41st Detachment to the Münchweiler Kaserne.

With Hooker and Merkins gone, I had the barracks room to myself. It was quiet, and I had a hard time sleeping the first couple of nights I was alone.

The barracks began to empty as soldiers were re-deployed or ending their terms of service. The warheads no longer on depot, the mission

9. Operation Silent Echo

in Fischbach had ceased to exist. The depot was a shell of what it once was, except for the 165th MP Company, who were still present.

Sergeant Kilgens began his move to the States. I shook his hand and gave his wife a hug. Even though I harassed him, and most likely got under his skin at various times over the years, I held a deep respect for him. Calling his 25th Infantry patch the "red hot chili pepper" or calling the rows of ribbons on his Class As the "fruit salad" was a way of me trying to approach him, not as a platoon sergeant and Vietnam Vet, but as a friend and man I could relate to.

Chief Vega also left for the United States. I really never got to know him, and I had the feeling he didn't really care for me. I may have been a little too wild for his liking, but I always attributed this to my being adventurous. I knew for sure he didn't like some of the other soldiers I hung around with, who were even more "adventurous" than me. He may have given me small signals of his disapproval, but I failed to pick up on them. I think he was trying to guide me indirectly, pointing me toward a path he believed would be more beneficial for my career, but I disregarded him. When he left, I didn't say goodbye. It felt like more of a relief with him gone.

We waited for our next set of orders, which Chief Boyd said would be coming soon. He only knew that we were going TDY to Ramstein and would be spending a month there.

Other nuke depots also began closing down. The 619th in Kriegsfeld closed, and I took a ride with Chief Boyd to pick up some equipment there. The MPs were still present at the site, but all of the bunker doors were open. I walked around the site with the chief, and it looked like a complete ghost town. In one of the empty bunkers, white powder covered the floor. I believed the WADS system went off in the bunker, and the white powder was the residue from the gas that was released.

The sight of the empty bunkers depressed me. 55Gs, from the 1960s to the present, were stationed here, each playing their role in the defense of western Europe. They came from all walks of life, and from every corner of the United States and its territories.

Now, Kreigsfeld was an empty shell of the Cold War.

10

The Final Days of the 64th Ordnance Company

We received the orders for Ramstein and packed up our equipment to make the drive. Since the TDY trip would be for a long duration, we would being staying in Air Force barracks on the air base.

The drive to Ramstein from Fischbach took about an hour as we passed through Pirmasens and took the Autobahn north. Being in the VW van without Merkins and Hooker to crack jokes had me feeling nostalgic for the past. Ruiz and Grogan were okay, but I was not on that comfortable a level with them as I was with my former roommates.

Chief Boyd drove the van, and Sergeant Preston was riding shotgun. They were discussing our mission in Ramstein.

There would be no projectiles to be disarmed; we would be working only with Pershing IIs, the warheads shipped to Ramstein from various depots throughout Europe that were not disarmed.

I started to question why they were not disarmed at the depots but shipped to Ramstein intact. We could only assume that the 55Gs in Italy, Greece and Turkey were also involved in the disarmament unless their depots were where these Pershing IIs came from. No one in the van knew for sure.

We proceeded through the checkpoint to enter the air base after being stopped and searched. Like other military installations throughout Europe, Ramstein had tightened security measures. Instead of typical army MPs checking our IDs and searching the vehicle, Air Force SPs (security police) performed this duty.

The air base was busy, with a constant flow of arriving and departing aircraft. C5 Galaxies, C-130 transport aircraft, and small fighter jets took turns taxiing down the runway.

10. The Final Days of the 64th Ordnance Company

The barracks we would be staying in looked more like hotels than airmen housing. They were bricked in a light brown color and had panel windows and beautiful grass-lined walkways to the entrance.

"Every year, the armed forces are given their budgets," began Chief Boyd. "The Army purchases rifles, grenades, tanks, helicopters, uniforms, helmets, Humvees, and everything else it needs to keep the mission on course. The Navy and Marines buy boats, planes, submarines, I don't know, ropes and whatever other junk it needs to keep *its* mission on course."

"The Air Force has a different mindset. First, it purchases things not related to its mission, like these big, beautiful barracks surrounded by maple trees, modern PXs stocked with the latest technological advances, and restaurant-quality food for their mess halls. By the time it is finished, it has no money left for runway repair, aircraft maintenance, sidewinder rockets, and whatever else it needs. It then received extra funds to purchase what it really needs to accomplish its mission."

Chief Boyd paused a second. "Now, tell me, who are the fools? We poke fun at the Air Force all the time, probably the same way that 11Bs poke fun at soldiers like us. But the airmen live comfortably and are probably being served steak at the mess hall this very minute, while we live in run-down World War II–era barracks, eating burgers as hard as hockey pucks in our mess hall." The chief looked at me laughs. I didn't know if he was pulling my leg or actually believed what he just said. But his words did make sense, and I could see by looking at the air base that he may be right.

We unpacked in our rooms, with Chief Boyd telling us to meet outside in 20 minutes for lunch. I was on the second floor with Sergeant Preston, while Grogan, Ruiz and Chief Boyd are on the first floor.

My room was quaint and had a latrine and wall sink, much like a motel in the States. There was a wall locker, writing desk, cloth easy-chair, and nightstand, which was next to the single bed. A half-length mirror hung above the desk on walls that are painted light beige.

I unpacked most of my belongings, stowing my BDUs and undergarments in the wall locker. My toiletries I took to the washroom, which had a small shelf below the sink mirror. I lined them up on shelf, then walked to the window.

Airmen were walking down the sidewalk in front of the barracks. They had a bounce in their step, and I watched as they playfully took a cap from one of their comrades and started to run away with it. The one who had his cap snatched from his head had airman stripes going up the length of his uniform sleeve. I never understood the ranking system in the Air Force and wouldn't have known how to address an airman NCO if I ran into one.

I met with the others in front of the barracks, Chief Boyd leading the way to the mess hall. The loud roar of aircraft engines was a constant barrage on the ears, especially the fighter aircraft that often flew in small squadrons.

The mess hall was busy, but the difference between an Air Force mess and an Army mess was quickly apparent. The floors were carpeted, for one thing, and the atmosphere was more that of a restaurant than a military mess hall. We got in line to eat, showing our IDs to an older man sitting at a desk at the beginning of the chow line. My mouth began to water at the thought of steaks and lobster, pork roast and au gratin potatoes; when we get to the servers, my dreams are quickly dashed. Hamburgers, sliced turkey, hot dogs, green beans, French fries, and mashed potatoes were on the afternoon's lunch menu.

I looked at Chief Boyd. "Steaks, huh?" I asked for a hamburger and fries.

This was my first lesson in military gossip, which was the same as all other types of gossip: most of the time the rumor being spread is false.

After lunch, we took our equipment to the secure site that would be used for our mission. We would be working in a small building, which consisted of one bay, a break room and a latrine. SPs were now providing security, and we were issued badges with our photos, which had to be worn at all times while on-site.

We began immediately, with Chief Boyd reading from the manual while we set up the equipment. I would be working with Grogan, while Sergeant Preston and Ruiz would be working together. The SPs had already lined the bay with Pershing II containers, and we began the process, slowly at first because I had not worked with the Pershings in Fischbach. Since the warhead was large, and its access panel easy to get to, we didn't need to take the warhead completely out of the container.

There was no designated tool person; we took turns between the crews using the tools to remove components from the warheads. The

10. The Final Days of the 64th Ordnance Company

process went quickly, and we began to improve our times each day. After the warhead was finished, the SPs pushed it out of the building. I didn't know where they were going, but I did know that they would be making their way back to the States for complete destruction.

The weekend came, and I hitched a ride back to Pirmasens with Chief Boyd and Ruiz. They spent the weekends with their families, and I spent mine with my girlfriend.

She asked me what we were doing in Ramstein, and I told her that we were working on vehicle modifications. She didn't press, and I offered no more information than what I wanted her to believe.

I did not go to Fischbach on the weekend but did meet up with some of the soldiers stationed there in the PX in Pirmasens. I asked them what was happening there, and one, an Specialist Carter, replied that people were being transferred to Husterhoeh Kaserne, Münchweiler, and other bases in Germany. Some were ETSing, and still others were returning to CONUS. The 165th was still there, but the 41st Ordnance Detachment barracks were completely empty. The bowling alley had also closed, and trucks and equipment were being moved off depot to other locations.

I told them to take care as I left the PX. I knew I would never see most of these people again, and it saddened me that things were changing so fast.

I took a taxi to my girlfriend's apartment with a grocery bag full of Combos snacks for her mother, who loved the small cracker and pretzel treats. I also had a bottle of cognac for my girlfriend, though I refrained from drinking this weekend.

Come Monday morning, we were in the final phases of our mission in Ramstein. About three warheads into our day, a man in civilian clothing showed up and stood near Chief Boyd. He was older, gray-haired, and he wearing a dark blue sweatshirt and faded blue jeans. He introduced himself, not saying his name, but only saying that he as an inspector. He also said his counterpart would arrive shortly and for us not to be alarmed, just keep working to complete the mission.

His counterpart showed up while I was taking a component out of the Pershing II warhead. I stared at him, just as the others were staring at him.

His uniform was gray with gold engraved buttons fastened in a perfect row up the center. He wore a round officer-style military cap with gold leaf clusters on the bill. His lapels were covered with a red-colored rank insignia, and he had ribbons pinned on the left side of his uniform. His black boots were tall and shined, reaching over his calves almost to his knees.

The man himself was of medium height, about 5'8", and of a thin build. His bushy eyebrows were gray and almost touched each other, like a unibrow.

The hammer-and-sickle pin on his uniform gave him away: he was an officer of the Soviet Union.

Though the Soviet Union had officially dissolved as of December 1991, its end of the INF Treaty had to be upheld. Just as the Soviet inspector was here to observe that the United States was upholding its end of the treaty, we had inspectors in the former Soviet Union observing its own operation of nuclear disarmament.

I was nervous as the Soviet stood over me, just to the left but close enough to see what I was pulling out of the warhead. I looked him directly in the eyes, and he smiled at me. I tried to smile back and found it hard to be pleasant with a man who was my enemy just six months ago. I did not trust them; it was just a feeling I had that someday in the future we would become enemies again.

General Patton wanted to go after the Soviets after World War II while they were weakened. He believed Stalin was intent on domination and the global spread of communism. Patton was called insane by politicians in Washington and the press. It took 47 years for history to prove him correct.

The animosity I felt is also related to being Croatian. Though Croatia was one of the five states of the communist union of Yugoslavia, the Yugoslavians in general held a contempt for the U.S.S.R., beginning with the Tito-Stalin split, when the Russians tried to control the politics of Yugoslavia. The president of Yugoslavia, Josip Tito, snubbed Stalin, and Stalinism in general. This action caused the expulsion of Yugoslavia from the Comintern (Communist International) in 1948.

My family were staunch anti-communists, and my grandfather helped relatives escape Croatia in the early 1970s by bribing officials to help secure their departure into Italy or Austria. The stories also instilled an anti-communist sentiment in me, and as I looked at this Soviet officer, those feelings begin to burn inside of me. I knew times were changing, and that we would soon no longer be considered enemies, as the

10. The Final Days of the 64th Ordnance Company

U.S. had won the Cold War. I believed wholeheartedly in peace through strength and wondered how the new Russia would deal with the last remaining superpower.

After the inspectors left, I forgot that I wanted to ask the American where he worked and if there were employment opportunities for veteran nuke techs. I searched for him shortly after we finished for the day, hoping he might be still in the area. To my dismay, he was nowhere to be found.

We completed the mission in Ramstein within two weeks and packed our belongings for the return to Fischbach. Chief Boyd informed us on the trip home that in one week we would be traveling to Hahn Air Force Base for the final phase of our mission.

The Fischbach Army Depot saw soldiers leaving weekly. Specialist Ruiz would be leaving before we traveled to Hahn. She was ETSing from the Army and returning to New York. I was never close to her, but I was sad that another 55G was leaving.

During the day, I spent most of my time in the barracks as we waited to leave for Hahn. We had no reason to return to the M&A building in Area One, as the it had been emptied of its contents.

The barracks were half empty, and I wandered the halls, hearing the echo of my steps loudly, when just one year ago, there were parties daily in the rooms on both floors, flooding the halls with music and loud bantering. I walked to the day room and found the soda machine still in operation but empty. The bottom button dispensed Budweiser beer for a dollar.

That evening, I hitched a ride to Pirmasens with an MP who happened to have one of the last remaining cars on depot. He maneuvered Thunder Road slowly, taking extra precautions to drop to second gear as he navigated the tight curves. I often took those curves at 40 mph, back tires sliding as I peaked over the cliff into the gulley below, then it was back to 70 mph on the straightaways, until the next curve.

We made Pirmasens, and I had him drop me off in front of McDonald's. He pulled away slowly, and I watched the Ford Taurus disappear around the corner.

Inside McDonald's I bought a Big Mac and a beer and took a seat at the front window. The Excezierplatz was directly across the street, and I watched as vendors who sold vegetables during the day began to close their shops for the evening. People were moving about, some going home, others to bars or restaurants, and still others, like myself, had nowhere in particular to go.

Not having people to hang around with was taking its toll on me. I wandered aimlessly around Pirmasens, stopping at small shops to browse, before making my way to Husterhoeh kaserne. I stopped at the NCO club for a drink and took a stool at the bar. There were crowds of men and women together at tables, talking and laughing it up, while I sat there a stranger, not knowing a single face in the building. I paid for my drink and left, entering Husterhoeh Kaserne proper, directly across the street. I showed my ID to the gate guard and walked leisurely to the bowling alley. I had never been in there, and it was very large compared to the two-lane alley in Fischbach.

The bank was also close by, and I walked there to take money out of the ATM in case I missed the bus back to Fischbach. The last bus left at 11 p.m., and when I got to the bus stop, I saw the schedule had changed, and the last bus now left at 10. I hailed one of the taxis which were always driving around the front of the kaserne and told the driver to take me to Fischbach. He was hesitant at first, since Fischbach is almost a 45-minute drive from Pirmasens. I showed him the cash, which made him feel more at ease, and he agreed to drive me.

I tossed and turned the rest of the night, though I had no nightmares. The quietness made it hard to sleep, so I ended up digging through my photo album the rest of the night. I found the photos of Hooker flexing in Paris, Switzerland, Verdun and Amsterdam. I saw photos of myself in front of the Crazy Horse in Paris and at the top of Dahnfels Castle. I was smiling in both photos, but I knew I was hiding the homesickness I felt during those times.

With Ruiz gone, Chief Boyd, Preston, Grogan and I traveled TDY to Hahn Air Base.

I called my girlfriend from a pay phone and told her that I would be back in a few weeks. Hahn was too far to be driving back and forth every weekend, but I would try to make it back if Chief Boyd drove to Pirmasens to see his family. My girlfriend was one of my last links to the area, and I did not want to lose that connection.

Hahn Air Base is located six miles from the picturesque town of Kirchberg, north of Pirmasens but also in the Rhineland-Palatinate. Kirchberg was an ancient town, known to the Romans of the 5th century as Dumno. It was called Chiriperg in the 7th century.

10. The Final Days of the 64th Ordnance Company

The town was well known for St. Michael's Church and a line of houses built in the *fachwerk* style. We passed through town, and I made a mental note to explore it as soon as I could get away.

If I believed the barracks in Ramstein were like motels, then the ones in Hahn were like the Grand Hotel. They were stunning structures, dark brown bricked buildings, completely modernized and built for comfort. I stashed my gear in a room on the second floor. Once again I had a private bathroom and furnishings.

Like Ramstein, we had to report to the SP station to have ID badges made. We needed to wear these as we entered and left the secure area.

The secure area was deep on the base, and to enter, there was a remote call button that one had to push and announce his intent to access the site. A soldier had to be cleared first, with the SPs having foreknowledge of his arrival. After speaking into the intercom, he was told to advance to the turnstile, which was of the same design as that in Area One in Fischbach. He was told to empty his pockets at the security window and to place the contents in a plastic container. I put in a cigarette lighter, coins (both German and American), and, as if solidifying a cliché, pocket lint.

The SPs spun the tray and my stuff disappeared inside of the building. They directed me to walk through the turnstile and to halt at the second window. I walked through, realizing that the Air Force SPs are all business. Without a smile, an SP spun the tray under the second window, returning my belongings.

Next, our equipment was thoroughly inspected, with every container opened and searched before being allowed to enter the area.

I signed in on the roster and waited for the others to pass through security. I took note of a sign put up at the gate opening to the secure site. "Cameras, weapons and recording devices are strictly prohibited from this point. Use of deadly force is authorized."

We were buzzed through the gate and walked to a storage building about 100 feet inside the site.

Like Ramstein, the building was full of containers, though this particular structure had two bays. We proceeded to drop off our equipment and set up the tool table in preparation for work the next day.

In the evening, I took the time to familiarize myself with the air base. There was a large commissary, a bowling alley called the Phoenix, and a fitness center on the base. At the commissary, I picked up *Soldier of Fortune* magazine and a small folding knife. I also picked up a loaf of bread, sliced cheese and bologna for the refrigerator in my room. I continued to walk around, amazed at the sheer size of Hahn Air Base.

It is close to 11:00 p.m. before I arrived back at my barracks room. I showered and went to bed. There was an awkward feeling to once again be sleeping in a strange barracks, and an air force one at that. The other 55Gs were staying in rooms down the hall from me, so I knew I was not completely alone.

After breakfast at the mess hall, we headed to the site. We went through the routine of gaining access, once again the unsmiling faces and monotone voices of the SPs guiding us through security. I had the folding knife clipped onto my belt and I gave it to them on the tray. They looked at it, passing it from man to man, then gave it back to me. I clipped it back on my belt and entered the site.

What we were doing in Hahn was a repeat of what was done at Ramstein. Chief Boyd read from the manual, and since we were working as only one crew, we took turns being the tool person. I knew the mission was important, but it became monotonous rather quickly and boredom soon set in. I refrained from drinking during the week, though, and reserved that pleasure for the weekends, if I could find someone to drink with.

Our daily schedule looks like this: we disarmed warheads, walked around the base trying to find something to do, went to German gasthauses for dinner in the evening, returned to the barracks, took showers and went to sleep. The next morning, we repeated the same process.

I started to bond with Chief Boyd during our time in Hahn. Once again, I bombarded him with questions about Korea. I wanted to PCS to Korea after Germany and asked him about the culture, the girls, the food, anything I could think of. I told him I wanted to re-enlist, but only if I could get Korea as a station. The chief promised to go with me to the 197th HQ building on Husterhoeh Kaserne to ask questions and start the paperwork.

It was late February 1992 and the mission in Hahn was almost complete. Counting the warheads in Fischbach, Ramstein and Hahn, we had disarmed close to two hundred nuclear weapons with only a dozen left.

We were on-site the final day, removing components from a Pershing II, when the chief discovered we had left a radiac meter in the

10. The Final Days of the 64th Ordnance Company

barracks and needed it to complete our work. He told me to drive to the barracks, get it, and come back quickly.

I rushed out, passing through security, and told the SPs I had to get a piece of equipment and would be back shortly. They gave me a nod and I jumped in the VW van and rushed to get the radiac meter. It took me a little more than 15 minutes to get to the barracks and return.

I was carrying the radiac and walked to the intercom. I pushed the button and an SP responded with a beep.

"Specialist Woodward requesting entry to the site." These were the words we were supposed to say every time we pushed the intercom button.

I waited. Silence. I pushed the button again. No reply. I pushed it again. A stern voice responded, "Back away from the fence! Drop the container! Take ten steps backwards with your arms up!"

I thought they are playing with me, so I hesitated. Suddenly, SPs came rushing out of the guardhouse, weapons drawn. I instantly dropped the radiac and put my arms up. One of them grabbed me by the upper arm and spun me around to face away from the site.

"Walk!" he commanded. I followed his order, freaking out about what was happening.

"What's going on?" I asked.

"Shut up!" he said. They pushed me toward a fence that was the first perimeter of the site. I heard sirens approaching fast and risked turning my head to see what was coming. An SP Humvee came speeding toward us, blue lights flashing and the siren on. There was an SP in the turret of the Humvee with an M60.

Christ, a little overboard, don't you think? I refrained from saying those words that were bouncing in my head and bursting to get out.

"On you knees! Keep your arms up!" I dropped to my knees, and an SP began to search me. His hands were rough as he grabbed parts of my body until they rested on something clipped to my belt. The SP ripped the knife away.

"He has a weapon!" I heard weapons being raised. By now, my legs were beginning to shake, more from anger than fear.

The SP that searched me commanded me to put my arms behind my back. I complied and he put handcuffs on me. I was then lead to the back door of the Humvee and forced to sit down.

We drove away. "This is just a misunderstanding," I told them. "I just went out to get a tool." They ignored me and continued driving. We stopped at the SP station and I was taken inside.

The station was empty except for a few airmen doing paperwork. They looked up at me, curious as to what was going on. I was told to sit down in a folding chair, and the handcuffs were removed.

"Your officer has been contacted and he is on the way," said the SP who frisked me earlier. I looked him in the eyes and couldn't tell if he as this serious about his job or just a jerk. I recognized him from the guardhouse; he was the one who gave me my knife back.

Time moved slowly until Chief Boyd arrived. He waved at me and then asked to speak to the OIC (officer in charge). He disappeared into an office around the corner, then returned minutes later carrying paperwork.

The chief pulled up a chair and sat next to me. "Sign this paper, then you can leave. It says you tried to access a secure site without authorization."

"But I didn't do anything wrong," I said, shaking my head. "They knew I left and was coming back. I told them I was leaving. I told them I would return. They're wrong. I ain't signing anything."

Chief Boyd pushed the paper at me. "Just sign the damn thing so we can leave. There is no way out of it. Do it." He handed me a pen, and I signed the paper. Chief Boyd turned it in, took me out of the station and drove me back to the barracks. I was beyond mad, and he knew it. He stayed quiet the entire drive, and when we departed to our rooms, he gave me sound advice.

"Next time, leave your knife at home." He smiled and entered his room.

The next day, our last at Hahn, I couldn't have been more thrilled. When we passed through security in the morning, there was a different set of SPs present. I avoided talking smack to them, as last evening's event had left a sour taste in my mouth about the Air Force. I bit my tongue and we entered the building to finish the last two warheads.

I looked at the last Pershing II lying there in its container. This would most likely be my last time seeing a missile warhead, and, rather childishly, I stooped down to kiss the skin of the missile.

We arrived in Fischbach, where Chief Boyd dropped me off at the barracks. He told me that I would need to start getting my belongings

10. The Final Days of the 64th Ordnance Company

together, as I was being moved to Münchweiler and had two days to get ready.

I walked down the concrete stairs to the EM club. There were three patrons present in a place that used to be packed on weekday nights with soldiers, their girlfriends, and family members. I took an empty stool at the bar and ask the bartender for a screwdriver. This bartender was relatively new, the wife of one of the MPs from the 165th. I didn't know her personally and had a hard time trying to strike up a conversation with her.

I took my drink to the back room, where the booths used to be filled with rowdy MPs and ammo specialists. I sat at one of the square, beer-stained tables, and looked at the slot machines, which to my surprise were still operational. I recalled when the British soldier tried to rip the arm off of the slot machine last year when he was drunk.

I pondered the fate of the depot as I sipped the vodka and orange juice from the glass with a tiny straw. Only 100 or so soldiers were left on the depot, and there would be no one PCSing to this station in the future. The dry cleaner closed down, as did Fritz's barber shop.

There was no doubt that the local economy would also suffer as a result of the depot's impending doom. Many military families rented housing in Fischbach, Petersbächel, Ludwigswinkel, and other surrounding towns. We shopped locally, buying consumables and foodstuffs at German butcher shops and bakeries. We also frequented local gasthauses and discos, spending money freely on alcohol and food.

The discos were also frequented by Americans. I decided to go to one last Rolling Disco Show before I moved to Münchweiler. It was held in Bruchweiler-Bärenbach, a town a few miles away from Fischbach, and I called Georg to pick me up Friday evening. I was happy to see him when he arrived.

The disco that evening was packed, and there were many familiar faces present. It felt like old times as I made the rounds, dancing here and there, doing shots with Germans I had not seen in months, and buying rounds of drinks for my friends there.

The music was loud, and the hall was packed with people. It's a wonder that no fights broke out, and in a rare, quiet moment, I noticed that I was the only American present. The soldiers from Fischbach that used to attend these discos on the weekend were long gone, and there was a feeling that a piece of the surrounding community was missing. The Americans had been present in the area since 1945, long enough to develop friends and family among the local population. I tried not to think of my missing friends and focused on having a good time with the Germans I also counted among my circle of friends.

I stayed at Georg's house for the weekend, and on Sunday afternoon he drove me back to the depot.

I finished packing my gear and personal belongings. I was told to take my sheets and bed coverings with me to Münchweiler. Chief Boyd arrived in the evening in his POV (privately-owned vehicle) to take me to my new home.

Reluctantly, I threw my bags into the chief's car. I took a last look around at the empty barracks, closed bowling alley, almost completely emptied motor pool with only a few trucks remaining. I listened to the silence, which, in its rudeness, had replaced the former sounds made by the soldiers of the 64th Ordnance Company.

We drove away in silence, and I looked at the sign that greeted me when I first arrived at the depot in January of 1990: "Welcome to the Fischbach Army Depot, Home of the 64th Ordnance Company."

I left a piece of me at the depot that evening, and I knew things would never be the same.

11

America or Bust

I was assigned a small, single room at the barracks in Münchweiler. These were the same World War II–era barracks that I was used to in Fischbach, far cry from the elegant dwellings that our Air Force brothers and sisters were housed in.

After putting my belongings away, I began a tour of the barracks, and I heard loud heavy metal music coming from behind one of the doors. I was about to knock and introduce myself when the door swung open and a tall, blond-haired guy was standing in the doorway. I recognized him instantly; he was with the 41st Ordnance and stationed in Fischbach before the company moved to Münchweiler.

"What's going on, man?" he yelled, obviously drunk. I couldn't remember his name and refrained from asking. "Wanna beer?" He pulled me into his room, where there were three other soldiers sitting around. They were playing cards, poker, I think, and looked up from their cards to see who walked in the room. I recognized them all, but once again, I didn't know any of their names.

I used to see this same crowd at the EM club on depot. They listened to the same type of music as we did, and the tall, blond-haired guy wore a jean jacket with a black Iron Maiden cut-out sewed onto the back. We partied with these guys a few times in their barracks, but never hung around with them outside of the depot.

I opened the beer and took a sip. "I just got transferred here."

"Well, welcome to the neighborhood!" said the blond. "We are having a party tomorrow night. Jungle juice, so bring some booze, doesn't matter what kind." I agreed to show up, and after finishing my beer, I told them I need to go. I still wanted to check out the kaserne and see what was here.

Münchweiler Kaserne was part of the Pirmasens military community and one of the medical facilities used by the Army. The kaserne had dependent housing for officers and enlisted personnel, a PX with a snack bar, a movie theater and a small chapel.

Before I first arrived in Fischbach, the bus made a stop here in Münchweiler. I went to the snack bar with the rest of the bus riders to grab something to eat. I wanted to try German beer, and when I approached the counter to order one and a cheeseburger, I became petrified. I was only 18 years old, too young to purchase alcohol in the United States, and I thought the law carried for U.S. soldiers here to Germany.

Apprehensively I stood at the counter, while a pleasant woman with black hair stood there and smiled at me.

"Can I help you?" she asked. She had an accent, though not as heavy as the German characters portrayed in American movies.

"A cheeseburger, fries and a beer," I responded sheepishly. The worker stared at me for a brief second, and I began to believe I had made a mistake. She began to ring up my order on the cash register.

"That will be $4.50," she responded, giving me the same smile. I walked to a table in triumph and enjoyed my very first authentic German beer.

Years later, while at my girlfriend's apartment, there was a knock at the door. When I opened it, I saw a black-haired woman standing there. She was smiling and said, "Hello."

I knew I recognized her, and it took me a while to figure out that this was the same woman who served me my first beer in Germany.

She also turned out to be my girlfriend's aunt.

Münchweiler was also close to the former storage facility of Clausen. Clausen was a tightly secured depot which stored 400 tons of VX and Sarin gas. Just before we began *Silent Echo*, in July 1990 Clausen began the process of removing the aging poison canisters from German soil. The depot had been kept a secret from the Germans for more than 20 years Fischbach was where the Germans falsely believed for years that poison gas was stored.

The U.S. Army, in conjunction with 1,500 German police officers, began the removal process with an 80-truck convoy, the first of 30 such transport operations, which would remove the canisters to another location 30 miles away. Helicopters followed the convoy, with snipers and sharpshooters guarding them. From there, they would be shipped

11. America or Bust

by rail to Nordenham, Germany, and put on specially-designed transport ships and sent to Johnston Atoll in the Pacific Ocean to be destroyed.

After the removal of the nerve gas from Clausen, I began to wonder how Georg and the Greens felt when they realized they were wrong. I still hadn't said anything about the nukes that were in Fischbach, as it probably would have given the locals a heart attack to find out their towns were sandwiched between nerve gas and nuclear weapons.

I had only two months until my ETS date, and Chief Boyd came to see me in Münchweiler. He told me he has something for me and handed me a green booklet. I opened it and aw a certificate inside. It is an AAM (Army achievement medal) for doing well during Operation *Silent Echo* and for helping the 64th Ordnance Company get excellent marks in the NWTI. I shook his hand vigorously and thanked him for the commendation. I knew it is only an AAM, and not very high on the medal list, but I was nonetheless thrilled to receive it.

Chief Boyd was PCSing to CONUS next week, but he wanted to take me to HQ to inquire about my re-enlistment options. I told him I was grateful and followed him to his car. The chief dropped me off, and aid goodbye, and left. He had to begin packing his belongings for his return to the States.

Husterhoeh Kaserne was still busy, with soldiers everywhere, performing whatever duties they were assigned to. I walked into the HQ building and met with an NCO about re-enlistment options. He went over my paperwork, marking a red line here, scribbling there, before he looked up at me.

"SPC Woodward, you don't have enough promotion points to deploy to Korea at the moment. In addition, the MOS 55G, Nuclear Weapons Technician, is being phased out of the Army. Your only option is to reclassify to another specialty."

"Well, I will only re-enlist if I get Korea as a station of choice." The NCO shifted some paperwork.

"The station of Korea we can't guarantee you. It will depend on what MOS you select and are qualified for. Your ETS date is July 25, 1992. That is only two months away. You also have 30 days of accrued leave. If you decide not to re-enlist, you can use your accrued leave days for an 'early out,' which will allow you to return to CONUS for out processing on June 25 of this year."

I became instantly furious. I didn't want to reclassify. I mean, what

Last of the Glow Worms

MOS could top being a nuke tech? Rather brashly I responded, "Just give me the early out."

"Ok, specialist. I will begin the documents. Also, in case you did not know, there is an option called European Out. You can ETS here in Germany if you plan on staying as a civilian. The Army will provide no assistance, though, if after your ETS date you decide to return to the United States. You will also be restricted from all military areas, including the PX."

I furrowed my brows; why the heck would I want to stay in Germany, then? I had friends here, and a girlfriend, but no employment options.

"No, sergeant," I replied. "An early out will be fine."

"I will get the paperwork going," he said. "Anything else of concern?"

I couldn't think of anything. "No, sergeant, that's it." I stood up and walk out of the office. The plans I had for a career in the Army were dashed before my eyes. How could I go from handling Pershing II warheads to being an 11B infantryman?

Within two weeks, Chief Boyd and Grogan were gone. The only ones left were Sergeant Preston and me. Since I stayed at the barracks in Münchweiler, and he stayed with his wife in off-base housing, we only spent a few hours together a day. I would take the bus to Pirmasens and meet him in front the HQ building.

We had no formations to attend, we didn't have to perform PT in the mornings. Truth was, we had no one to report to. We usually ended up hanging out in the bowling alley on Husterhoeh Kaserne, talking about former times in Fischbach or about our families back home.

I began to stay weekdays at my girlfriend's apartment so I did not have to take the bus to Pirmasens from Münchweiler. During this time I became closer with her siblings, which forced me to perfect my German to be able to hold a conversation with them. They asked me about Chicago, which lead to the inevitable questions about Al Capone. My answers seemed to satisfy their curiosity, which changed the subject to music. We all ended up having relatively the same tastes, metal, house music, techno, etc. Her brother introduced me to German rock, which I quickly became fond of.

After conversing with them for an evening, I realized that we are not so different, the Germans and Americans. We had the same desires, dreams and hopes for the future. We had families we loved and wanted nothing more than to live peaceful and happy lives.

With two weeks left to my ETS date, I decided to give Georg a call to hang out with him one last time. He arrived at the barracks on Saturday afternoon and drove to a small bar in Dahn.

The bar had a few patrons, who nodded to us when we arrived. It had a counter lined with stools and a row of booths against the front window. In contrast to the older-style gasthauses, this bar was more contemporary, with modern paintings hanging on the white walls and red vinyl seats for the booths. It was quaint and modern, a representation of the new German generation that had arisen from the ashes of the old.

We took a place in one of the booths at the window and ordered a "meter board," a three-foot-long piece of flat wood with holes cut through the bottom that held 10 glasses of beer. I asked them to make it Park Dunkel, a dark, smooth pilsner.

"Prost!" yelled Georg, and we each downed two beers as quickly as possible. The beer was room temperature and slid easily down my throat. I put my head back and felt my face flush.

We talked and drank the day away, and when he realized he was too drunk to drive, Georg called his sister to drive us back to his house.

Georg's sister was married to an American at one time and had a child with him. They divorced soon after and she moved back in with Georg and his parents. The child was four years old and did not speak English. I had tried to speak to him in the past, switching between English and German, to see if he could tell the difference. He went to his mother and told her, "I can't understand what this man is saying."

The next afternoon, I had Georg drive me back to Münchweiler. When we got there, he got out of the driver's seat and came around to my side of the car. I got out and took his hand, knowing this was probably the last time that I would see him. I pulled him in and hugged him tightly, like old comrades, and we slapped each other on the back. Despite myself, I fought back the tears that I could not let him see. I told him goodbye and stood in front of the barracks, watching his car drive away until it disappeared on the road behind the chapel.

I began out processing the week before June 25. I was given a checklist to follow, which began at the supply room. The first day of out processing, I brought my duffle bag full of gear to the supply building. I gave the specialist there my checklist and he sorted through my gear.

"One Kevlar helmet, one LBV, one NBC suit, one gas mask, one set of NBC boots, one canteen, one tent half with stakes...." He read down his list, inspecting my gear and marking off check boxes on a piece of paper.

"All right, man, you're done," he said, signing my checklist. I thanked him and left, going to my next appointment. I planned on getting as much done as possible the first day so I could spend quality time with my girlfriend before leaving.

At the community headquarters building, I made an appointment for my personal belongings to be shipped back to the States. The lady behind the counter informed me of the appointment for the movers, which would be in three days, between the hours of 8:00 a.m. and 4:00 p.m. She also asked me if I had any car plates to turn in, which I responded to in the negative. I handed her my checklist and she signed off.

I headed to finance next, to terminate my direct deposit. The clerk checked to see if I had any outstanding debts, which I didn't, and gave me my ticket for a flight on Delta Airlines on June 23 departing from Frankfurt International Airport and arriving at JFK International Airport in New York City on the same day. Next I walked to the bank to close my account. I had my savings put into a cashier's check which I had mailed to my parents' home in Brookfield, Illinois. I took out the money from my checking account in cash and some of it changed to German marks.

The first day of out processing, I completed my entire checklist. I only had to wait for the movers to come.

To my surprise, the movers showed up at 8:30 a.m. I had just returned from the mess hall and was barely in the door when they arrived. They started taking my belongings downstairs and to a moving truck. It's not that I had much, just a stereo system, clothes, beer steins and souvenirs from the places I visited, and tons of books. I watched them pack my stuff, and when they finished, I was given a receipt with every item listed.

"How long will it take for my stuff to get to me?" I asked the man who handed me the receipt.

"Three months from today," he responded. "Slow boat to China."

I had two days until my flight home. I arranged with Sergeant Preston to pick me up at 5:30 a.m. at my girlfriend's apartment for a ride directly to the airport.

11. America or Bust

I spent the remaining time with my girlfriend. In the evening, I joined her, her sister, and her cousin at a nightclub in a nearby town called Lemberg to have a small going away party. My girlfriend knew the owner, and it was usually quiet on the weekdays.

The club was darkly lit, except for the rotating blue and red lights that bounced around the dance floor. It had a ambiance to it, like that of a nightclub from the 1950s, where one could find gangsters huddled in a corner booth discussing illegal activity. There were about 15 people in the club, some of them on the dance floor, and some at the bar. I had never been to this club and noticed something strange—all of the patrons were men. I looked at the dance floor and saw men dancing together, the disco ball spinning colored sparkles on their clothing. I then took a look at the bar and saw men sitting there, sharing drinks, their stools turned in pairs to face one another. They leaned in close as they talk, laughing and putting their arms around each other's shoulders.

I looked at my girlfriend, who quickly realized what I had just picked up on.

"We know the owner. He is a good man. Don't worry. *Du brauchst keine angst zu haben."*

I tried to push the situation out of my head and focus on having a good time. My girlfriend told me it was not a gay club, just that the owner was gay, and these were his friends. I could only think of what Hooker or Merkins would say if they found out I was here on this night. They would've had a field day, and by the end of it all, the whole depot would have known.

We drank into the night, and I shared fruity cocktails with my girlfriend, listening to her sister and cousin try to converse in English, which sent me over the edge in laughter.

I looked at my girlfriend, her blonde hair which she wears long and straight, blue eyes on a face that is typical German, and a nicely shaped body, which stands just under 5'7". She wore a black bra under a mesh top, a tan mini-skirt, and knee-high suede boots. I watched her as she moved her body to the music, swaying back and forth in the booth.

I decided then and there that I would marry this woman one day. I didn't know when or how, I just knew I would. It was the same feeling I had before I decided to enlist in the Army; it was a calling, something I felt inside. The same feeling drew me to this woman.

The night of my departure came, and we stayed up most of the night, recalling the past and talking about the future. We sat on a small, plush love seat for two people. I held her and told her that I would see her again. I promised that things were not over between us. We would meet again. I fell asleep in the chair, and it seemed like only moments before the alarm went off. Groggily, I slowly got dressed and had a cup of instant coffee. My girlfriend woke up just in time for Sergeant Preston to honk his car horn under the window. I gave her a firm hug, repeating the words from last night: We will see each other again.

Sergeant Preston and I spoke little on the trip to Frankfurt. He was PCSing soon and reclassifying as a 95B, military police. During the ride, I wrote down my address and phone number and asked him to please stay in touch.

Frankfurt International Airport was hustle and bustle, and Preston stopped in front of the Delta departure terminal. I grabbed my duffle bag and shook Sergeant Preston's outstretched hand. We made promises to stay in touch, and with a heavy heart, I entered the terminal.

The flight back to the States got diverted to Iceland when a passenger suddenly became ill. We landed at Keflavik International Airport for the sick person to receive medical attention. I looked out the window and saw low-lying fog covering light-covered patches of grass, the landscape broken by rocky crags. We waited two hours, and the plane took off for JFK.

I traveled by bus from JFK to Fort Dix, New Jersey, for out processing from the military. I scanned the skyline of New York City and saw the Statue of Liberty in the distance, holding her torch high, beckoning the disenfranchised souls from around the world to come and seek a better life. I thought of my great-grandparents who had arrived here from Croatia and the hope and fear they must have felt when they saw Lady Liberty 70 years earlier.

I was put into a small barracks with 20 other soldiers who were ETSing. We were assigned cots and the room was rambunctious and full of mirth as the soldiers prepared to go home permanently.

The day's schedule was full of filling out paperwork, which was finished rather quickly, and ended with me getting a plane ticket from Newark to Chicago's O'Hare International Airport.

I hadn't seen this part of Fort Dix when I did basic training here

11. America or Bust

three years ago. I looked at it differently now; through the eyes of an experienced soldier the base looked less threatening than when I was a raw recruit in 1989. I walked around and took in the sights before returning to the barracks.

In the barracks were some soldiers who were involved in a scuffle at the airport. One of them had his head wrapped in a bandage and the other had a splint on his right forearm.

They told us they were jumped by thieves at Newark. A staff sergeant was with them and he began to address the room.

"For safety, please travel in a group." That was all he said, and I assumed that this was the first time he had dealt with a situation like this.

On June 25, I took a bus from Fort Dix to Newark. We arrived at the departures terminal four hours early. I was with a group of five soldiers, and we decided to stretch out on the floor for a few hours in a group to lessen our chances of being robbed.

I arrived in Chicago at 12:30 p.m. on June 26, 1992. The sky was gray as we made our approach; I had hoped for blue skies and bright sunshine to mark my arrival.

My brother picked me up at O'Hare, driving a 1977 brown Cutlass Supreme. He was two years younger than me and had enlisted in the Army as an Apache helicopter mechanic. We drove the pothole-filled 294 toll way south to Brookfield.

My father was home when we arrived. I hugged him tightly and began answering his questions about the trip. He said I could stay here as long as needed, until I found a place of my own.

I took my duffle bag upstairs to my old room. It looked exactly the same as when I left. I plopped onto the twin bed, folded my arms underneath my head, stared at the ceiling.

I accomplished what I set out to do, chiefly making it through three years in the military. I did not see combat, did not deploy to the Persian Gulf, and did not "engage" an enemy on a frontline. I nonetheless felt proud that we, the "glow worms," the invisible men and women who maintained the U.S. Army's tactical nuclear arsenal from the early 1950s until 1992, sustaining the mission of nuclear deterrence in both Europe and Asia. We handled weapons capable of destroying entire cities and performed our duties with diligence and pride. We came from all walks of life, from the low income neighborhoods of Brooklyn and the farmlands of southern Indiana to the suburbs of Chicago and Pittsburgh.

We were on a different frontline, the one that divided the enemies of the Cold War and their allies into two camps, NATO and the Warsaw Pact. As we were disarming our nukes in Europe, there was a counterpart in Russia performing the same task. I think about a young Russian soldier, in his late teens or early 20s, removing components from an SS-20 Saber tactical nuclear missile under the watchful eyes of an American inspector. I wonder if he had the same feelings of hope, or possibly fear, at what the future held for our two nations.

Our mission accomplished, the threat of nuclear war diminished greatly with the collapse of the Soviet Union. The minute hand on the Doomsday Clock has been set back, giving the populations on both sides a moment of reprieve from the threat of nuclear annihilation.

Epilogue

Like most veterans, when I came home, I realized that nothing had changed. The neighborhood was the same, and the friends I had before I left for the military were either in college or working. When I got together with them, I quickly came to the conclusion that I had lost something I had in common with them in the past. They couldn't understand what I did in the Army or the experiences I had while traveling throughout western Europe.

In August 1992, I applied for a position at the Argonne National Laboratory in Lemont, Illinois, as a radiation specialist. Argonne was a nuclear research facility at the time, and I thought I would be a "shoo-in" for a position. I put on my resume that I had experience with nuclear weapons, radiation monitoring, and safety procedures.

What I quickly learned, though, is that without a master's degree, I had no chance of gaining employment at Argonne. I then enrolled in a staffing agency and found that positions in the civilian world pertaining to nuclear weapons were nonexistent. I ended up taking a minimum-wage position with Wells Fargo as a security guard. I also enrolled in college to take advantage of the G.I. Bill and Illinois Veterans Grant.

I kept in touch with Hooker, who was attending a university in Pennsylvania. In 1993, I drove there to meet him, and our reunion was joyous to say the least. That would be the last time I saw him in person.

In 1994, I married my German girlfriend, who had decided to join me in the United States. We had a small, civil ceremony in Chicago and stayed two years until we decided to move back to Germany. I found a job in the construction industry and even worked with a crew of Germans to renovate one of the barracks buildings in Baumholder. I felt a wave of nostalgia wash over me; just six years prior, I was there at the range, qualifying with an M60.

Epilogue

In 1997, the German company I worked for was contracted to rebar the foundation of a new biosphere reserve that was being built in Fischbach. I was excited; I had not seen the town since 1992.

What I first noticed in Fischbach was the obvious lack of Americans and everything that used to cater to Americans. There had been an Esso gas station where Americans filled up their vehicles using gas stamps purchased at the PX to avoid paying German taxes. The gas station was still there, but the signs in English were missing. The same went for sandwich boards in front of cafes or gasthauses. With the Americans gone, I was sure the local economy took a hit.

The city of Pirmasens had also changed. The reduction of American forces in the area had caused a change in the small city's economy. The Burger King closed down, and for a short time the chapel was a dance club. The barracks at Bunker Hill, which once housed the bulk of American families stationed in the Pirmasens military community, became low-income housing and, later, housing for refugees and asylum-seekers.

The departing Americans turned over control of Husterhoeh Kaserne to the Germans on June 15, 1994. A museum was located in the "banana building" and numerous German car dealerships and other small companies were now located on the former kaserne.

All other U.S. Army installations in the area were also closed, Camp Dahn, Münchweiler, Massweiler, and Clausen. The Germans took custody of all former installations and converted them to civilian use.

The former Area One on the depot in Fischbach, where we housed and maintained nuclear warheads, had become a Cold War museum in 2012. The rest of the depot contains businesses and a solar farm. A gasthaus was located in the former bowling alley and the old theater became what is was designed for.

The 59th Ordnance Brigade was officially deactivated on October 15, 1992. On October 1, 1994, the brigade was reactivated at the Redstone Arsenal and merged with the United States Army Ordnance Missile and Munitions Center and School (USAOMMCS). The commandant of the school also became the brigade commander. In 2002, the school was renamed the U.S. Army Ordnance Munitions and Maintenance School/59th Ordnance Brigade.

In the United States, the 832nd Ordnance Battalion was moved from Redstone Arsenal, Alabama, to Fort Lee, Virginia, on July 26, 2011.

The legacy of tactical nuclear weapons in the U.S. Army has a history spanning nearly 50 years. The elimination of the weapons systems by the United States and Russia (then the Soviet Union) helped stabilize Europe and alleviate the fears of hundreds of millions of Americans and Europeans. The threat of nuclear war waned, and the legacy of Operation *Silent Echo* went down in history as one of the largest leaps of peace between the United States and Russia.

My heart goes out to the young men and women who battled and still battle in Iraq and Afghanistan, facing a new type of enemy, one that doesn't wear a uniform or have large bases of operations. The soldiers of today are facing threats that we did not have during the Cold War, suicide bombers, IEDs, child warriors, and enemies hidden in plain sight.

I hope one day that peace will prevail over malice, and the need for young men and women to fight, and ultimately die for their country, will one day cease to exist.

References and Further Reading

Websites

http://www.ig-area-one.de The Cold War museum, located at the former site of Area One. Run by Horst Himbacher and Rolf Birnstein.

www.usarmygermany.com A comprehensive website of information and stories pertaining to American Forces in Europe during the Cold War. Run by Walter Elkins.

Publications

Corry, John. "TV: Pershing II and West Germany." *The New York Times* 28 December 1983.

Department of the Army Pamphlet 50–5. *Nuclear Accident and Incident Response and Assistance (NAIRA) Operations.* 20 March 2002.

Fields, Joseph A., Lieutenant Colonel OD. *Tactical Nuclear Weapons Responsibility: Ordnance Versus Field Artillery.* 8 March 1990.

Pincus, Walter. "Army Spending $35 Million to protect Nuclear Arsenal." *The Washington Post* 26 January 1984.

Vogel, Steve. "U.S. Details Plan to Remove Chemical Weapons from Germany." *The Washington Post* 9 March 1990.

Index

Amsterdam 110–111, 160

Brookfield, IL 9, 16, 91, 172, 175

Crazy Horse Saloon 76–77, 160
Croatia 84–85, 92, 102, 109, 119, 134, 158, 174

The Day After 4

832nd Ordnance Battalion 178

Fort Dix 17–18, 21–22, 49, 174–175
41st Ordnance Company 52–53, 56–57, 106, 120, 135, 152, 157, 167
Frankfurt 44, 46, 108–109, 172, 174

Gorbachev, Mikhail 133
Greece 1, 6, 14, 36–37, 135, 154
Greenpeace 136

Hahn Air Force Base 135, 144, 159–162, 164

Intermediate-Range Nuclear Forces (INF) Treaty 4, 6, 133, 135, 158

Kriegsfeld 44, 135

Lance Missile 6, 35, 37, 44, 53, 64, 66, 131–133, 144, 147, 149, 152

M31 Honest John 6, 33
M422 5, 36
M454 5, 35–36, 64, 71, 113, 130, 131–132, 142, 147, 149
McDonald, Congressman Larry 5
Münchweiler 49–50, 143, 145, 152, 165–171, 178

NAIRA Exercise 126–127, 142
Nicholson, Major Arthur 47

197th Ordnance Battalion 47, 49, 55, 135
165th M.P. Company 52, 56, 79, 87, 90, 120–122, 127, 135–136, 148, 153, 157, 165

Operation *Paperclip* 32
Paris 74–76, 78, 141, 160

Patton, General George 3, 48, 103, 158
Pershing II 1, 35–37, 53, 55, 64, 66, 74, 131–133, 144, 149, 152, 154, 156–157, 164, 181
Petrov, Stanislav 5
Pirmasens 47–50, 52–54, 90, 97–98, 100–102, 107–108, 111–112, 122, 135, 145, 154, 157, 159–160, 167, 170, 178

Ramstein Air Force Base 55, 90, 105, 135, 140, 144, 147, 149–150, 153–154, 157, 159, 161–162
Reagan, Ronald 4, 133
Red Army Faction (RAF) 105, 113, 125, 137
Red Dawn 4
Redstone Arsenal 30, 32–33, 38, 49, 130, 179

Silent Echo 1, 133, 140, 141, 168, 169, 179
Soviet Union 1–2, 4–6, 47, 135, 158, 176, 179
SS-20 Saber 5, 36, 133, 176
Stalin, Joseph 158

Tito, Josip 158
Turkey 1, 6, 33, 36–37, 118, 135, 154

Verdun 75, 78, 160
Von Neuman, John 2
Wertheim 123
Wuerzburg 113–114, 123

York, Sergeant Alvin 3
Yugoslavia 102, 134, 158

www.ingramcontent.com/pod-product-compliance
Ingram Content Group UK Ltd.
Pitfield, Milton Keynes, MK11 3LW, UK
UKHW042014140426
5217IPUK00015B/1175